"Long Ago, No One Called My Name"

Y MORRIS

Scripture quotations are from the NIV, KJV and New Living Translation Holy Bibles. Research on Google.com; BibleGateway.com and Biblehub.com

Photo Credits:
Front cover picture taken by Ina Jean "Cookie" Metty
Back cover picture taken by Steven E. Morris

Copyright © 2018 Yvonne Marie Beltran Morris
All rights reserved.
ISBN-10: 1720618879
ISBN-13: 978-1720618874

Thank you JESUS for loving me first and creating me, so that I may appreciate Your death on the Cross, which gave me eternal Life in Your Kingdom.
You alone are my Father, my Mother, my Sister, My Brother, My Family.
Thank You for showing me the path to eternal Life. I thank You that You never gave up on me! You continued to "knock" on my door and I am grateful that no words, but the reading of my heart reveals to You, how deep I love You.
Thank You for entrusting me with Your message to my beloved brothers and sisters who are lost. I know I am but one of many believers You have opened our mind to know Your coming.
JESUS, as You know, I can hardly wait to drink wine with You and eat at Your table!

Thank you Husband, Steve E. Morris, for being my punishment, lol in the heart! An inside joke between my love and me. I truly am grateful with tears in my eyes that you are a man of moral character when it comes to being faithful and loyal to your spouse. I will see you in the Kingdom of GOD brother.

DEDICATION

This Book is dedicated to the fearful and unbelievers, as placed in my heart by GOD. Above all important to me in life, is deliverance of one soul to the Kingdom of GOD. Remove yourself from earthly drama, issues, and materialism. What matters? Nothing matters, but being one with the LORD GOD JESUS. The Lake of Fire, and hell is real and Heaven is real. Hear. JESUS has contacted each one of you and made His presence known. He, JESUS, offers peace and salvation to us all, take it now. **Repent** and **Believe, GODISJESUSLIVES**.

CONTENTS

CHAPTER 1   11
GROWING UP WITH EVIL; ROMAN CATHOLICISM AND LUCIFER

CHAPTER 2   24
PRESIDENT DONALD J. TRUMP CHOSEN BY JESUS
FOR HIS GRACIOUS PRESIDENTIAL SEAT
ROBERT MUELLER AND HIS LUCIFERIANS BATTLE WITH GOD

CHAPTER 3   39
DO YOU WANT TO KNOW THE TRUTH AFTER YOU DIE?

CHAPTER 4   53
DO NOT BELIEVE EVIL SPIRIRTS PRETENTDING TO BE HOLY
ANGELIC SPIRITS

CHAPTER 5   66
JOSEPH PRINCE GOSPEL OF GRACE; JESUS BOYS AND GIRLS

CHAPTER 6   78
JESUS APPEARED
DARKNESS FLEES WHEN LIGHT APPROACHES
IVANKA TRUMP AND GRACE

CHAPTER 7   91
ONLY TWO CHOICES, ETERNAL LIFE WITH JESUS OR ETERNAL
HELL WHERE EVERYONE IS A BELIEVER IN JESUS

CHAPTER 8   104
ARE YOU SURE YOU ARE GOING TO THE KINGDOM OF GOD?
FEDERAL PRISON WITH FAITH IN JESUS

CHAPTER 9   117
THE GRACEFUL FIRST LADY MELANIA TRUMP
REPENT AND BELIEVE IN JESUS

CHAPTER 10   132
THE RAPTURE WITHIN 14 YEARS; ARMAGADDON SOON
JESUS IS COMING IN MY GENERATION

INTRODUCTION

I thought about it. That's true. We always called Grandma when Dad was beating Mom up, or when he was beating up older sister. Grandma would come in the middle of the night after a frantic phone call from one of us kids and calm him down.

Grandpa would drive her over to our house and not say a word. He just stood quiet, with his cowboy straw hat. She was the only one who Dad respected in his drunk. Immediately Grandma would scold him in Spanish and he would refrain from being evil. She only spoke Spanish. I love my Grandma who is [1]asleep resting in peace.

While l was looking in the mirror I asked GOD, "why do you even care about me, a horrible person like me? Why waste your time with me?" All of a sudden, GOD said, "compassion."

The LORD actually answered me. Then I said compassion huh? I asked GOD, "where were You when my Mom was getting beat up by my Dad everyday and molesting my older sister?" Again, plain as day JESUS said, [2]"Daughter, no one called My name."

GOD then flashed in mind all the hundreds of times; we called Grandma to settle her son down from his drunken rage, terrifying us all. GOD was right, not once did we call upon GOD the Father or GOD the Son, JESUS.

We didn't even acknowledge GOD or give thanks to GOD except after meals. Mom would always have us say, "thanks be to GOD" after every meal.

---

[1] 1Thessalonians 4:13

[2] Jeremiah 29:12-14

It became something to say without really feeling or hearing what or to whom we were being thankful.

That was the extent of our GODLY family. We didn't even have a bible sitting out. We never turned to GOD for anything individually or as a family.

Sure, we went to Church lots of Sundays. Sure, we attended catechism. Sure, I had some Roman Catholic schooling and confirmation for communion in 1971, but we never called on the LORD as a family.

Wow!!! Our LORD GOD called me, "daughter." He called me, "daughter." I am GOD'S daughter. Immediately I checked to see how many times in the Gospel, did JESUS call a woman daughter.

Only once, JESUS turned and saw her [3]"Take heart, daughter, He said, your faith has healed you." The woman was healed at that moment. Healing is always at that very moment with JESUS.

At an early age, I knew of a spiritual world. I never doubted GOD existed, but I had only met demons in my childhood. How thrilled I am to have JESUS call me "Daughter." I wasn't expecting an answer from GOD. I was talking to myself I thought. I write this book with the authority of JESUS and He tells me what to write.

Here is the message from JESUS. Call His name. Call on JESUS for help. That is what He told me, "Daughter No One Called My Name" and that is true. We never called on GOD for help. Today's sermon (June 10, 2018) from Pastor Frank was that message; we need to call on GOD for all healing and all help.

---

[3] Matthew 9:22

GODISJESUSLIVES

GODHSELVES

1

Growing up with evil
Roman catholicism and lucifer

I was born June 20, 1964 in Refugio, Texas, which periodically hits Father's Day. Refugio is located at the foot of Corpus Christi, Texas. As a baby, I recall the feeling of protection. When I was 9 months old laying next to my Mom's bosom, an overwhelming feeling of love and protection existed. I remember little children in the room looking upon Mom and me, feeling no harm can come upon me. These are true feelings and thoughts as an infant. At 10 months old, I remember taking a bath in the kitchen sink. The summer wind blew warm, while I sat in front of the only window in the in front of the kitchen sink. I can still feel the wind and happiness attached to that comfort of joy.

At youth, only evil spirits showed themselves. I did not see JESUS or feel His presence until my adulthood. The first time I recall encountering spiritual evils was at age 4. I was taking a nap with my Mom. I woke up to my 8-month-old sister performing fellatio on me. I remember the expression on my sister's face when I looked under the sheet to see what was happening to me. I made eye contact with my baby sister. I saw an unusual expression on her face with a gesture of laugh. Her eyes looked at me with a spirit of pure immorality. [4]I did not know the devil or one of his evil followers could posses a child's body. A demon had entered my baby sister. Sister and I were innocent children not knowledgeable of sexual acts or evil spirits.

---

[4] Matthew 9:32-33; 12:22; 17:18

I never told anyone until recently. I knew it was wrong and I was left confused. I cannot put into words the distress placed upon me by this demonic force. I do not want to embarrass or hurt my baby sister I love her. She does not know this evil occurrence. We never spoke about it and I wish not to hurt her but let you all know what demons can do. I am sure my brother and sisters, along with my Parents have occurrences of repulsive evil acts they experienced. Looking back, violent, sexual, and unholy evil spirits tormented my entire family.

Another early encounter as an innocent child was at the age of 4 3/4 years. I was taking a nap with my mother, my sister and both pet dogs, Baby and Brownie (miniature half Chihuahua and Poodle). I was laying face down with my feet hanging over the bottom edge of the bed. All the sudden, I awoke to the bed shaking frantically. I looked at my Mom, my sister, and my dogs for some reaction. They were sleeping peacefully. I could not believe anyone could sleep while the bed is bouncing and shaking violently.

Then the devil made physical contact. The devil clawed my little feet that were hanging over the edge of the bed. It was abrupt and frightening. Instinct of the reflex immediately pulled the knees to chest. Totally scared and confused, I woke my Mom up and told her what had happened. Mom was groggy and showed no concern. She said it was probably one of our pet Chihuahua dogs that had probably clawed my feet. I told her they were on the bed. She continued to sleep. They all continued to sleep. I knew it was evil had done that. I did not go back to sleep. I laid in bed scared.

The feeling of long claws by something not human was supported by pictorial thoughts by the devil. Demons tormented me with frightening thoughts. They threw those frightening thoughts into my mind as a child.

When I rode with my Grandma and Grandpa all over South Texas searching for medical treatment that would help my uncle Andres. Every time I rode in a vehicle, devils would put thoughts of a grossly scary beast with claws followed me on the pavement behind the vehicle.

First grade was at Our Lady of Refuge, a Roman Catholic school. It closed before I could attend second grade, as did my two older siblings. I was the only Spanish child in my grade. Dark in complexion, I stood out. I came home from school one day and leaned against the wall in my bedroom, looked upward and blasphemy JESUS. I had to be possessed, as I did not know JESUS well enough to like or dislike him.

The profanity was vulgar. I was wearing my plaid gray and blue uniform skirt with a white blouse. I can see myself, a little 6 year old Roman Catholic girl leaning against my bedroom wall and looking upward cussing JESUS. I said very nasty vulgar profanities towards JESUS. I did not yell, but spoke knowing JESUS heard. [5] I am certain a demon entered me as a child and blasphemy JESUS then left.

I do not know why demons are aloud to possess children and I have never asked our LORD GOD. Read the story in the gospel about the [6] Greek woman (gentile, not a Jew) who showed JESUS her faith in Him as GOD. It is told in the gospel: The woman was a Greek, a Syro-Phoenician by birth, and she dept asking Him (JESUS) to cast the demon out of her daughter.

But JESUS said to her, "Let the children be filled first (children meaning the Jews) for it is not good to take the children's bread and throw it to the little dogs." And she answered and said to Him, "Yes LORD, yet even the little dogs under the table eat from the children's crumbs."

---

[5] Matthew 15:22

[6] Mark 7:26

Then He said to her, "For this saying go your way; the demon has gone out of your daughter." "And when she had come to her house, she found the demon gone out, and her daughter lying on the bed."

Grew up not knowing what[7] salvation meant. Did not know the meaning of JESUS' death on the Cross. Did not know I was on the path to eternal hell. I did not know what I had to do to avoid hell by choosing life with Joy eternal. I did not know I was born with sin. I thought just believing in GOD would get me into the Kingdom of Heaven. I was a very shy little girl growing up. My parents and us children have always believed in GOD and JESUS, but we did not know what Grace was, nor did we repent for our sins and change our ways.

We did not pray at home. No family bible sat out in our house. No GOD or biblical stories shared at home. No prayers prayed before meals, or at Thanksgivings. My Dad was a drunkard; a wife beater; a child molester most his adult life. He held the same job for 30 years and provided for his family of four children and a wife. We were low-income family, yet we lacked nothing. Dad was a hard worker. His dark side was when Dad would cut, hurt and devastate Mom or my sister.

Dad would physically assault Mom or older sister, followed by verbal assaults, weekly. I remember Mom crying and crying with my baby sister sitting on her lap, Dad had sliced her shoulder with a knife about seven inches long and an inch deep. She let it heal on her own, as she did all the time, never going to a doctor. There was a time I had hate for my Dad and placed a needle on a chair in hopes he would sit on it, but Mom did and I felt awful. I think I was only eight at the time.

---

[7] 1Thessalonians 5:8

All I knew was I was born in Refugio, Texas and my Parents and Grandparents were Tex-Mex, but all our birth certificates said "white". Well I thought, Mom said we were "Spanish," so I thought in the 60's, Texas only recognized white or black. The color of my skin is dark brown. We didn't speak Spanish only English. Parents only spoke English to us.

Knew of the word [8]"voodoo." Mom put red rose-colored pedals in brother's bath water so he can win his track meet race. I remember Roman Catholic priests blessing our home with holy water several times. Dad always cussed some spirit he said was an old lady who died there tormenting him. Astrology, horoscope reading is evil. Stay away from horoscope reading daily and physic places unless you have chosen to be a luciferian (new word). Targot card reading is evil.

How GODLY blessed that, I did not attend a Roman Catholic school, as did my brother for eight years and my older sister for five years. Roman Catholic leadership teaches their own rules and cause innocent children, women and men to become sickly, sometimes deadly. Roman Catholic religion is a ritual. They don't teach the Gospel of Grace. They allow worshipping of idols and praying to statues of women and men who were created by GOD. They call them saints! Well understand this all you believers in JESUS, we are all His saints.

We will judge the evil fallen angels created by JESUS and locked up in the middle of the earth in chains. The Vatican is evil. You do not need Popes as interceders. Popes do not take the place of JESUS. Know this Pope and all Roman Catholic leaders, you are no more important to JESUS than me, than President Trump, than most of my fellow brother and sisters at the Martin City food bank.

---

[8] Galatians 5:20

If you Roman Catholic leaders are not right in the heart with your fellow believers, then you are not allowed to take communion. What moral example are you showing your congregations? Looking back, I see what a fool I was. Oh sorry LORD JESUS, you say to never call anyone a [9] fool. Have mercy on me LORD.

When I was I think age 9, I went to bed and woke up to many, many demonic eyes starring at me. I cried for Mom. She did not know what to do. Mom took me to the other bedroom, but that did not stop the phenomenon of demonic eyes terrorizing me by the hundreds. Pairs of demonic eyes were around and above me in layers and layers occupying with ease our 9 x 10 bedroom. I was able to see a supernatural dimension of thousands of demons in that small room.

Only flipping the light switch on would remove them from my sight, but when I closed my eyes, I saw them in my mind. The demon's eyes were the dullest blue, yellow or red where the white is in our eyes. The demons had large black circles where we have eye color. The ugly slant of the evil eyes where 3 to 6 inches in length, and 2 to 4 inches in height. I felt the demons were laughing at me and enjoyed terrorizing me. I also felt they existed before me and different in size and power. I had the wisdom to know GOD was not causing the evil I saw of a starving kid like me on television. That event led to my first thought of why GOD? I have never blamed GOD for anything
foul or ill happening.

Had we only known we could command these evil spirits to leave our home and us alone by the name of JESUS? Demons tormented, and influenced me, and family members older and younger than me. Weird and evil things would occur in our home. In those days, vacuum cleaners had a metal flip switch to turn them on.

---

[9] Matthew 5:22

One evening I was watching television with Mom when we heard the vacuum cleaner come on. Vacuums were loud back then too. Mom had a look of confusion and a touch of fright. Mom did slowly go turned it off.

When I was 12 or 13 years old, for two weeks I was too scared to sleep. I would wake up unable to speak or move my body. I lay there paralyzed and unable to scream out to my Mom for help. Demons tormented me with scary thoughts of death being final. That earth continues without me, never again experiencing life. That once I die, that was it for my existence. All kinds of evil and confusing thoughts would arise in my head. Total "darkness" told me, by demons for weeks. The evil spirits had me fearful of death. Demons were putting dark thoughts in my head. All kinds of evil lived in the home I grew up.

I began my evilness at an early age. That was when people started to compliment my outside beauty. I was black on the inside. I was the best manipulator. I felt I could get in a person's head easily. I was materialistic. I was a great liar and darkness was my path. I chose evil because of pride and greed living within me. I was not to deceive; I chose to become a deceiver. I was a product of a dysfunctional home with no GOD. With all the evil, sexual and physical assaults, all immoral act, family that functioned. I thought my deceptions would not hurt anyone but me, if truth surfaced.

Even then, prove it first. Of course, I did not see the ugly in me. I put no thought into deception being evil. What harm could it bring deceiving others to better one? I was born family centered, not self-centered. Everything I did was in hopes of bettering my family's life. Never have I had sex for money or to further myself. Never promiscuous and never cheapened; that alone, does not separate us from filth.

Attracted to opposite in appearance, found the man I wanted with blonde hair white skin educated and on his way up. At age 22, he had his new home, car, and motorcycle and flew airplanes. Graduated at age 17 from high school, premeditated pregnancy and thrilled to the pain of others. Gee, I never thought of consequences. We married and have a daughter. He deserved better. That marriage led to traveling to Europe, Japan and other countries. I surrounded myself with luxury. I chose my physical beauty to further worldly lust. More corruption and more manipulations, I was deeper into darkness.

Then history repeated itself when I placed my daughter into Our Lady of Perpetual Help, a Roman Catholic school in hopes she would get a solid foundation of who JESUS is (although I was not walking in the light) was a waste of money and precious time. The entire time married to her father, another Roman Catholic, we owned not one Holy Bible (Gospel of the Kingdom of GOD), nor did we ever speak to GOD as a family. Worldly people we were a worldly family of the earth, but empty inside and lusting for all the world could give us. He did say one thing that remained in heart about GOD. He said to turn to GOD not only when things go bad, but also when things are good. In Roman Catholic schools, you don't learn "Through His (JESUS) name, whoever believes in Him will receive remission of sins."

To all brothers and sister who believe in JESUS but do not understand what it means to repent and filled with pride. Pride only hurts you in the realm of Heaven. Change yours ways. All readers believe in JESUS. GOD loves you just as much as GOD loves those who are saved. To be allowed in the Kingdom of GOD, you must change [10] your ways by repenting. Understand forgiveness as explained by JESUS. Are you above Our LORD JESUS? Will you not forgive your fellow believers'?

---

[10] Matthew 18:21-22

[11]"You will know them by their fruits." [12]Are you a good bearing tree or a bad-bearing tree? Let GOD and not your evil flesh control your actions. I have to tell myself this often by repenting and asking JESUS to control my behavior. I need His power to help me quite often. Repent means to change your evil ways, forever. I am grateful that JESUS cares and knows my heart. Thank You LORD GOD JESUS. Praise GOD. Amen.

Most Roman Catholics don't even know what the Holy Bible says. Most Roman Catholics don't even know they are hurting themselves by taking communion every Sunday or Wednesday. Have Communion everyday if you want, but you must be right with GOD to do so or Communion will have ill affects upon your body. Communion is not a one-time event. Communion for me is a constant event, a divine habit. You become rejuvenated.

You don't need a priest or pastor to take Communion. It is between you and GOD. The same with being saved and born again, you don't need a pastor or priest. Immediately when you are forgiven by the blood of JESUS CHRIST and born again, you are saved and a child of GOD.

Not all Popes or pastors and priest are saved. Praise the LORD. GOD renews many people's youth, including my own. JESUS who fills us up with rejuvenation of love and it shows in our youthful and vibrant appearance. His glory shines upon us. Communion releases many miracles. GOD wants you healthy. JESUS took the bread and said take it (chew it) "this is my body" "drink now this is the cup of the New Covenant, my blood."

Speak this truth and honor JESUS when you have Communion. There is power in JESUS.

---

[11] Matthew 7:15-20

[12] Luke 6:43-45

Take some grape juice or whatever you drink and use it as a symbol of the blood of JESUS. His blood was shed for the remission of sins, past, present and future. Drink it in remembrance of the New Covenant JESUS has with all.

The Old Covenant is gone; we are no longer under the law. GOD said, "I will remember their sin, no more," under the New Covenant. We are saved by, Grace. JESUS is put into remembrance as we drink His blood and eat his body.

Holy Communion heals us. JESUS is a healing GOD. There is no purgatory like (my former religion), the Roman Catholics believe. Don't be misled by, Roman Catholicism. You will only end up in hell if you think there's purgatory.

Again, there is no purgatory. JESUS tells us all there is the Kingdom of GOD and there is the pit, hell where suffering is everlasting. GOD has told us we can't pay for our sin. The price has been paid by, JESUS. We cannot pay a price for salvation. You cannot earn your salvation. Do not be fooled. Our blood is not sufficient to pay the price for salvation. Only our creator JESUS' blood paid the price for our salvation. The blood of JESUS is purely divine.

JESUS paid the price for our sin. First you must not have any hate, unforgiveness (new word) or unbelief in JESUS as the Son of GOD. Examine yourself before communion by looking into your own heart and attitude. Ask yourself, "am I right with the LORD?" "Am I right with my fellow believers'?"

All you Roman Catholics who have ill will towards President Trump, Vice President Mike Pence, any believer in JESUS cannot partake in communion. Check yourself to see if you are free to partake. If the answer is no, you must withhold because you would then be eating and drinking condemnation.

The Pope and his Roman Catholic leaders need to teach their congregation that the Gospel of Grace states, "But let a man examine himself, and so let him eat of that bread, and drink of that cup. For he that eat and drink unworthily, eat and drink damnation to himself, not discerning the LORD'S body."

Have the right attitude before you have communion. You can become sick and weak, even death (fall to sleep) if you are not right with the LORD. [13]Otherwise, if they are not or no one is teaching the Gospel of Grace then they are cursed times 2.

Getting right with GOD, the LORD is, understanding what is wrong, sin is wrong. Acknowledge your sin and humbly confess it to GOD, "for it is with your heart that you believe and are justified, and it is with your mouth that you confess and are saved." Repentance is then accomplished with your faith in JESUS. Confessing "JESUS is LORD and believe in your heart GOD raised Him from the dead, you will be saved." Faith is necessity. The pope doesn't teach this. P.S. You can have communion at home. You don't need a priest or pastor.

Roman Catholic priest don't teach this. Roman Catholic members are ignorant to the scriptures of Truth. You too Mr. priest who was on Fox news during St. Patrick's day thinking its ok to drink beer. I pray for you. I pray for all you lost souls in the name of JESUS. Few people are saved; and surpass pastors and priest in knowledge.

I am certain that most people of the religion I was raised in have never read the Holy Bible otherwise they would quit praying to Virgin Mary who was human and not divine. She was blessed among all women and chosen by, GOD for her heart.

---

[13] Galatians 1:8,9

Evil angels appear all the time to nuns from the Roman Catholic religion posing as Virgin Mary, making them believe she is the way. JESUS is the only way. No other way but through and in JESUS can you be saved.

The sincere Jews and sincere people in other religions who practice their faith without accepting JESUS are going straight to hell after their first death and upon judgment, their second death. JESUS says this not me. Don't worry about other points of arguments with other believers of JESUS.

What matters is we are all saved. People from the Muslim, Hindu, Roman Catholics, Baptist, Jews, who have the faith in JESUS and believe in JESUS, will be saved from hell. Following religion without the faith in JESUS is the path to hell eternal. There is no salvation apart from faith in JESUS CHRIST. There is no other way to heaven. Having faith in JESUS is how you save yourself. Repent and belief in JESUS is not a religion but spirituality.

I follow CHRIST JESUS, therefore a Christian. JESUS is LORD. You may be following your faith in believing in GOD, but without faith in JESUS you will still go to hell. Sincerity in religion is not enough, but the faith in JESUS is what is most important to us creatures of JESUS.

Overcome this world and it is false condemnation and guilt. JESUS saved us. Now save yourself by choosing eternal life with GOD. Righteousness is a gift. Save yourself by accepting JESUS as the Son of GOD, whom was sent by GOD to die for our sins on a cross.

JESUS is our Savior. JESUS is Lord and died for us all. JESUS took our place on that cross. GOD imputed all the sins of the world into the body of JESUS CHRIST and bore all our penalties, curse, and judgments. Once, and for all, JESUS died for all sins of the world we thank GOD our Father for JESUS' sacrifice.

JESUS CHRIST is our Lord and Savior now and forever. We thank GOD in the name of JESUS. Amen. This is Grace. This is the mercy of JESUS. It is your own soul, your own heart, and your own destiny to choose. [14] "Only fools say in their hearts, "there is no GOD." They are corrupt, and their actions are evil; not one of them does good!

---

[14] Psalm 14

2

PRESIDENT DONALD J. TRUMP CHOSEN BY JESUS FOR HIS GRACIOUS PRESIDENTIAL SEAT

ROBERT MUELLER AND HIS LUCIFERIANS' BATTLE WITH GOD

The first encounter I had with JESUS was in 1996 when He began speaking to me. I was not saved and still an immoral creature of GOD when JESUS began using me as His instrument. I was in my early 30s when JESUS told me to [15]"faith heal" this man named Mike who had been in a serious car accident that left him in a wheel chair. When the Lord JESUS speaks to me, it was not audible. It is clear and true. GOD uses few words deep meaning. This was the first miracle JESUS had me participate was in rainbow bar, Kalispell, Montana.

I was not looking for JESUS or hiding from Him when he had me "faith heal" this guy named Mike. I felt bashful inside knowing I had to say to initiate a way to approach Mike and tell him "he did not have to believe in JESUS, but that what I am about to do is being done in the name of JESUS." I was stalling and JESUS was nudging me to do approach him. I am shy with people, but apparently not so with JESUS. I said, "ok." I also said, "Ok, ok, ok."

I said to Mike (who happened to sit next to me, "you do not have to believe in JESUS but this is in the name of JESUS." I began to surface his [16]wrist without touching him and whispered, "in the name of JESUS" for about a minute.

---

[15] Acts 9:4-5

[16] Mark 3:5

I could feel his pained area. I could feel where his body suffered releasing funnels of energy.

I did not tell anyone about the "faith healing" in the beginning. I did not even know what "faith healing" meant, but JESUS told me that I am a "faith healer." A few days later, I saw Mike at rainbow bar and he told me that while on his way home after the "faith healing," he experienced a burning sensation in his wrist followed by complete healing. I said, "Lets do your legs!" I surfaced his legs while he sat in his wheel chair claiming quietly, [17]"in the name of JESUS." Mike healed, completely.

Then while in a casino a lady approached me and asked if I could go to her home to heal her. I did not know her but she had seen me faith healing a woman's head. I did go to her house. Again, JESUS told me to say that she did not have to believe in JESUS but that the healing was in the name of JESUS. She began to vomit and healed of her illness.

[18]I was in the Spirit of GOD when I went to my Mom who was in a wheelchair because of diabetes both her legs we amputated below the knee. I walked into my sister's home, got on my knees and surfaced her right eye while I said, "in the name of JESUS". I saw and witnessed to transparent white matter the size of dandruff immediately spit out of her right eye, then her left eye. I thought,[19]"fish scales." The thought those little white yet transparent particles were "fish scales" entered my mind by JESUS.

Mom grabbed me by my hair crying and said in Spanish, "daughter, never did I think I would see your beautiful face again." Her sight healed and restored.

---

[17] Acts 3:6

[18] Revelation 1:10

[19] Acts 9:18

I walked away not knowing what had just happened and did not know she was going blind or having serious vision loss. I gutted a little fish at Lions Lake on Father's Day (June 17, 2018) and there they were, those little transparent particles I witness spit out of my mother's eyes.

For a while, JESUS had strangers approach me for faith healing or I would Faith heal others led me by JESUS. In all things is the [20]name of JESUS. Amen. Spiritual occurrences, unexplained knowledge entered my life in spurts from that point. I remember seeing this poor young boy in agony lying in a hospital bed and I raised my hand from the hallway towards him and said, "In the name of JESUS" and instantly he laid there peacefully.

Healing in the name of JESUS is instant. It is instant! I had proof that JESUS heals and lives. He spoke to me. Yet, my behavior was same and continued on dark path. Yet, I was ignorant of what it really meant to die in darkness. I was clueless. I was unaware of choosing from the only two choices we humans have. Unaware and careless, acknowledge the "two choices" of truthful destiny. One destiny leads to torment filled darkness.

The other destiny leads to joyful loving Light. I did not even think about my destiny. I felt I would live and be beautiful forever on earth.

In 1997, I asked my former husband on the other side of the country, "Who is this Bill that keeps tapping into my [21]"sp here?" Again, I was in the Spirit of GOD when I asked him an out of the ordinary question based on nothing ever spoken of and no knowledge of what is a sphere and how it relates to man.

---

[20] Acts 3:7

[21] Job 26:10

I do not know what possessed me to ask him such a question based on no information from man regarding "Bill" and "sphere". He told me he had been speaking to a medium named William Perry. [22]All mediums consult or possess by an evil demon or demons pretending to be a Holy Angel/spirit.

According to people, William Perry states his childhood spirit friend is "Dr. Guiseppe, a 16th century psychiatrist."[23]I did not know at the time I was speaking to a devil, a high-ranking devil who knew my families entire past from the beginning of time on earth.[24]Bill was from St. Louis Missouri and in the process of establishing some kind of spiritual retreat. My former husband asked me, if I had been haunted as a child by demons. Wow, I was shock with that question. I never told anyone what I experienced as a child, yet he knew details.

I told my friend Pat and she was intrigued and asked if I could get his number. When I called my former husband for the mediums phone number, got it and said thank you. He stated he had not given me the number. I repeated the number I had just written and it was correct. He was puzzled claiming he had not yet given it to me, however it was Bill's number.

Pat asked I call Bill with questions regarding her deceased husband. I was reluctant but did.

This medium Bill immediately went into a different character with a strange voice, which stretched the words he spoke. The devil posing as Dr. Guiseppi immediately spoke to me about my future (lies, lies, lies), mentioning he knew me from Heaven. That we knew one another from a university in heaven and that we studied with one another.

---

[22] Leviticus 19:31

[23] 2 Corinthians 11:3-4

[24] John 12:31 & John 14:30

He mentioned that I was in my fifth stage of life and that my name was majesty in heaven. So what do I do, I get an email named majestyvonne. What trickery and lies the devil used on stupid me.

Stupid, naïve, egotistical, and sinful, I was arrogant. I had not read the WORD yet or knew anything Biblical. The devil is slick and speaks half-truths. JESUS is Majesty. I fell into that trap laid out by that devil of many. My ex husband told me he heard the tape recorded by Bill and given to the people who call him, for a donation he gives his services. My ex husband said never has Bill spoke to anyone of his clients that he knew of, regarding spiritual or supernatural statements.

Surprisingly, the spirit left bills body after our session. [25] Know that demons and the devil use evil trickery filled with half-truths and many lies. They are experts at deceiving the flesh, and easily they do. [26] They have been around before JESUS came the first time, as a Man.

The devil and demons know our ancestors and watch generation from generation manifest and die. [27] They know our family tree. They know heaven, GOD and JESUS. They know the [28] "Kingdom of Heaven" and the Holy Scriptures in the Holy Bible. They know hell is their past, present and future. They want all of us humans to burn with them eternally. JESUS central message to us was,[29] "Repent, for the Kingdom of Heaven is at hand."

---

[25] John 8:44

[26] 2 Corinthians 14:14

[27] Luke 10:18

[28] Genesis 1:1

[29] Matthew 3:2

Only GOD knows why He allowed me to briefly move into that home. Do you hear me reader. I am witnessing that GOD is our CREATOR and JESUS is GOD and lives. Truth is JESUS. [30] Knowing I tell true, choose life, not hell. Choose eternal life and not eternal hell. JESUS told me to tell all, GODISJESUSLIVES.

I went to church yesterday (May 20, 2018) and Pastor Frank gave a great sermon on what Anne Graham comment on years ago after 9/11. GOD spoke through her when she made awareness of all the school shootings and how people wonder why GOD allowed this to happen.
Think about all the luciferians who were able to remove GOD from our schools, prayers from our coaches and players. You really think GOD wanted to leave? You really think it was an act of GOD killing these believers and non-believers?

Why would GOD not want the will of His children to be prayers in schools and GOD acknowledged? Yet we blame GOD when he allows evil to take over and removes His protection from schools. Again, Pastor Frank topped his previous sermon. He continues to do so every Sunday. People who live in the Flathead Valley, especially Columbia Falls, Hungry Horse, Martin City and Coram, attend Active Word Ministry, 5091 US Highway 2 W., Columbia Falls, 406-892-0587 a Grace Gospel church filled with the Holy Spirit of GOD.

Pastor Frank is a compassionate and big-hearted Pastor doing the preaching he was called to do by JESUS. His tears and love for the Body of CHRIST is real and true.

I presently have to either listen to 880 AM radio news or go over to a friend or mother-in laws house to watch TV news. I have been unable to pay Dish Network the $176.00 I owe them for four months now.

---

[30] John 14:6

Just last week JESUS blessed me with $179.00 to pay towards a $605.00 Flathead Electric bill and was matched $203.00 by Energy Share and another $200.00 by F.E.C.

I could go on and on about the blessings and faith I have in JESUS, but this is about JESUS and His coming soon to gather His children in the clouds. This book is about salvation and how it is a gift to all people, simply repent and believe in JESUS. GOD is good always.

Speaking of a friend, Praise GOD I have true Christian sisters. Donna who lives in Martin City and married to Tom are true righteous children of GOD. Donna is a person all people should have in their life, a caring and loving JESUS girl. Thank You JESUS for Donna.

Understand this all you so called Christians and leftist liberals, haters of President Trump, Sarah Palin, even Sean Hannity (GOD'S children), if you don't remove the hate from your heart, you cannot partake in communion. You cannot have fellowship with GOD. The truth is you will become sick or die.

All you so called leftist, heed the warning from JESUS. JESUS speaks to me all of the time Joy Behar and others who think its ok to play around with their eternal destiny. Continue hating GOD'S children. Continue to choose not to believe in JESUS, the Word of GOD. It is union with JESUS that we live and breath.

Not with CNN the mother to all fake news. Not with the Vatican filled with treasures that could feed all the starving children and people in this false world.

[31] Robert Mueller, James Comey, Rod Jay Rosenstein, Andrew McCabe, Sally Yates, James Clapper, and that deep dark state those white supremacy old white men John Brennan are playing with the security of our country, which are Obama's puppet master.

---

[31] Matthew 7:9

[32] They are all in a fight against, GOD. All will lose this war. "...But if it be of GOD, you cannot overthrow it; lest perhaps you be found even to fight against GOD..." Look how GOD is exposing them. lucifer is going to continue to use them and does not care if they are imprisoned or die and go to the "Lake of Fire" made for him. They are luciferians. Father, In Your Name JESUS I pray you remove the darkness shielding Your sons eyes and bless them with the knowledge of hell, so they may repent and believe. Amen.

I must say this Kanye West, a son of GOD has had a JESUS moment and does not want to be separated from his mother, or his children in the Kingdom of GOD. Don't worry about this William guy who thinks he can judge you. I love you Kanye as a sister to a brother in CHRSIST. JESUS will soon correct this Will Black eyed...

Stephen Hawkins suffered on earth and shall suffer hereafter eternally. Believe me, he met JESUS the moment he died. That was a big bang non-theory. Father, In Your Name JESUS I pray that Your son Stephen called out to you before his death and repented in his heart out loud to you before he took his last breath. Amen.

People do not be fooled by who really ran the government while Obama was President of the U. S. A. The deep state allowed Obama to play with executive orders and with the White House. He was their puppet and did a good job not to rock the boat. Keith Richards, you are no voice in "the wilderness" so uppy shutty. Worry about your spiritual destiny, repent and believe in JESUS. Call JESUS.

I am proud of Dennis Rodman and believe him to be a JESUS boy. Jeff Ross, go home and retire. In addition, you're a white guy pretending to be black at the Rob Lowe Roast and every roast since its conception.

---

[32] Acts 5:39

I have Northern and Western African in my blood, and laugh at your hate. You apologize Jeff, to sister Ann Coulter. She too is a JESUS girl.

"I am black baby, music will never leave me, but I am leaving you." JESUS gave me this lyric twice in a vision and it is heavenly when sang in a female voice with dramatic angelic orchestratic music I heard (April 2018). There is hate where you are heading, but no laughter. Repent now Jeff and believe in JESUS. Your time is near. Kanye I give you the above heavenly lyric.

Before Donald J. Trump became President, I wanted Ted Cruz to win because of his constitutional commitment and the fact he too was Texan and JESUS boy. Trey Gowdy, a good JESUS boy who would be an ultimate choice Supreme Court Justice-that is where you would shine. Father in the name of Your Son JESUS I pray you continue to shower Your son Trey with unmerited favor and Grace.

In January 2016 as I was watching Fox News (I began watching the news when Trump entered the elections. All others news stations were deceiving the country, especially CNN) I started to compare Trump to the Rich man and Lazarus story in the Gospel of Grace (Holy Bible) then JESUS stopped me as I was writing this into this book and told me Trump was going to be president of the United States of America.

It was His will to put Trump in "His Presidential Gracious seat." I quickly changed my tone and obeyed Our LORD GOD'S will to use Trump as He willed. All you haters of our President Donald J. Trump are haters of JESUS. Don't you know, don't you know it was JESUS, who allowed the evil deep state to use Obama's evil character only to use President Trump's righteousness in GOD to expose the truth? You can't fight and win against GOD. All you people who laughed at the recent journalist dinner at the White House are angering JESUS.

"Daughter, No One Called My Name"

Remember how JESUS made Obama and that little comedian who poked at Trump during that same dinner eat their words. JESUS allowed tainted mud in their face. Mc Cain should have love for Trump equal to the lust he had for me when he saw me at the Scottsdale airport in the early 90's. What makes him hate President Trump so easily as a Christians? Does he not fear GOD? Donald J. Trump's presidency is not of human origin.

John Brennan and Robert Mueller are at war with GOD. [33] "And will not GOD bring about justice for His chosen ones, who cry out to Him day and night?" I am a mighty woman of GOD and I cry out to JESUS for justice now regarding Brennan, Mueller and all white supremacists as they, including their puppet Obama, continue to waste taxpayer's money. Samantha you have no powers.

So what if President Trump called that gang "animals." JESUS called Pharisees "you snakes! You brood of vipers! How well you escape being condemned to hell?" You luciferians causing trouble for GOD'S President Trump should concern yourself with your own soul and where your final abode shall be. You are at war with JESUS, not President Trump and you will lose to your Creator, JESUS. Repent and believe in JESUS.

All you luciferians, haters of President Trump, it is JESUS' Will to have him (Trump) as an instrument, doing work for GOD. JESUS will say to President Trump and all his children doing His will [34]"well done, My good servant!" Grace saves us, but it does not please JESUS to hurt Him when we hurt one another. Father, In Your Name JESUS I pray the chains of hate be removed and replaced with love in the heart of your son john. May he understand Your Will. Amen.

---

[33] Luke 18:7

[34] Luke 19:17

JESUS tells us all there is the Kingdom of GOD and there is hell, separation from GOD, if you don't repent. Your spirit will be thrown into the "Lake of Fire" where suffering is everlasting. We are under a New Testament established through JESUS. We are under a New Covenant through the blood of JESUS CHRIST.

In the Old Testament, animals were sacrificed for the covering of sins, while under the law. GOD gave us JESUS who laid His life down freely to cover our sins, with His divine blood. All sins were brought to an end at the cross. JESUS bore the full payment of our sins, our children's sins and onward. JESUS said, [35] "It is finished" at the cross before returning to GOD the Father.

JESUS is where we are at all times. JESUS is everywhere. He is a wonderful Holy GOD. All in the galaxies, universe obeys JESUS. We need to do the same. It is our self-righteous disobedience to JESUS that caused pain and suffering in our lives. The world will be set in righteousness and we will have Heaven on earth with JESUS as our King, our Lord. JESUS is the only Hero. There are no heroes but JESUS. He is our Hero. Worship JESUS. Do the will of GOD and be with JESUS in the end times and eternally. Believe in the gospel of Grace and believe in JESUS. Proclaim JESUS CHRIST as your personal Savior and Lord, today.

Again, JESUS woke me up with thoughts of messages of information for His book. Atheists have chosen to not believe in Him and thereby choosing already believes in Him, but pride gets in their way. Most atheists believe in His existence. luciferians and atheists have chosen to be mad and filled with pride to not repent.

---

[35] John 19:30

Which reminds me of the sad spirit in the non funny girl at the White House correspondent dinner is truly a Wolf who's destiny is the "Lake of Fire" where she will have all eternity to sorrow about her short moment idolizing recognition and false love by others. Father, In Your Name JESUS I pray she open her mind and heart to Your Truth and repents and believes in, "For GOD so loved the world that He gave His only begotten Son, that whoever believes in Him should not perish but have everlasting life." Amen.

Sean Hannity is a son of GOD. He is truthful and a great servant of the LORD GOD JESUS. Father, in Your name JESUS I pray Your glorious light surrounds Your son Sean, his family and all those he loves and prays for. Amen. If former President Bill Clinton, truly repented and believes in JESUS, then he is saved, and enters JESUS Kingdom.

Great is the fact that at death he shall part from Hillary. In marriage, woman to man (GOD does not recognize the abomination man to man or woman to woman in or out of marriage) they become one flesh, but always two separate spirits. I witnessed the transformation of President Trump rebirth in CHRIST JESUS. He is saved and will have eternal life in the "Kingdom of GOD", the "New Jerusalem," His wife and family too will be his brothers and sisters in Heaven on Earth. Fox News and Newsmax are JESUS based news channels.

CNN is like, Not Hillary x2, fake, untrue, liars not allowed in the Kingdom of GOD, unless they change their ways by repenting. Hillary, JESUS was never going to allow you to be President of the USA.

The evil done by Obama, Brennan, Clapper and the other luciferians were allowed to show the Glory of GOD. This country does not want you either as a leader of any sort. Repentance is then accomplished with your faith in JESUS. Father in Your name JESUS I pray Your daughter Hillary finds the lighted path to salvation. Amen.

Confessing "JESUS is Lord and believe in your heart GOD raised Him from the dead, you will be saved." Faith is necessity. If you are a believer and continue to sin in the eyes of the Lord, JESUS revealed to Paul, you will be chastised (disciplined).

If you are not disciplined for your continued sins, then you are not the children of GOD and not saved. If you think you are saved and continue to sin in the dark, then you are a child of the devil.

The devil was created as we are created too. JESUS, who is GOD the Son, our Lord and Savior, created angles that chose to be evil which are fallen from the Kingdom of GOD. We call those fallen angels devils. Fallen angels have sinned and cast out of Heaven by GOD.

Fallen angels are created spiritual beings that rebelled against GOD. Demons, in my opinion, are the evil spirits of [36]"Nephilims" ("The Nephilim were on earth in those days—and also afterward—when the sons of GOD went to the daughters of humans and had children by them.") and those "mighty men" fathered by sons of GOD with human daughters of GOD. [37]"the sons of GOD saw that the daughters of humans were beautiful, and they married any of them they chose."

The main one is lucifer, the demon leader. The New Testament mentions the devil (satan) 36 times in 33 verses. "That ancient serpent, who is called the devil and satan, the deceiver of the whole world," thrown down to the earth with the other angels that rebelled against GOD. "For you are the children of your father the devil, and you love to do the evil things he does.

---

[36] Genesis 6:4

[37] Genesis 6:1-2

He was a murderer from the beginning. He always hated truth, because there is no truth in him. When he lies, it is consistent with his character; for he is a liar and the father of lies." "Then he said, "You son of the devil, full of every sort of deceit and fraud, and enemy of all that is good! Will you never stop perverting the true ways of the Lord?"

The hypocrisy that exists is thick in this world. All over the world we live in hypocrisy. My Christian neighbor, ridiculed me for backing up my vehicle politically incorrect. She lives across the street with the Ten Commandments on her home. Her anger was with JESUS and not me at the least; she just did not know demons threw thoughts to condemn me and I have seen it happen with others.

She text me the following: "I pray in that in the here & now the Lord will Bless you all not to feel the need to drive across your neighbor's driveway instead of in the road the Lord has blessed us with! This is my thought, not from Patti." [38] Do not judge, and you will not be judged. Do not condemn, and you will not be condemned. Forgive, and you will be forgiven." Every believer better heed the words of our LORD GOD JESUS.

This same neighbor would not place her hand on a Holy Bible because her [39] "no is no and her yes is yes"... beyond swearing, yet she lied about having a key to her future ex times 2 just had made. I thought about how she believes what the evil neighbor says; yet she lied in court...was Judge Heidi J.Ulbricht to believe her, although she lied?

---

[38] Luke 6:37

[39] Matthew 5:37

Heidi is my Christian friend and deserves the truth from other JESUS girls and JESUS boys. I left the courtroom confused and hurt for Heidi when it should have been hurt for JESUS. I know I am a sinner; I had her on a different level, but taught we all try and fall short. This should teach us all not to judge others and not to be gullible either. We are all same. My Ten Commandment neighbor, a Sabbath keeper, 7th Day Baptist is saved and a JESUS girl. She is my heavenly sister. Amen.

3

DO YOU WANT TO KNOW THE TRUTH AFTER YOU DIE?

It is Grace, which reminds us all, JESUS died for not only our past sins, but our present and future sins too. It was Grace that totally vanished me from a video…I kept telling JESUS how I did not want to lie, but did not want to be put in a position where I might lie.

For months I kept telling JESUS this and He knew my heart and the weakness of my flesh that He removed my presence from a video that the devil was using to make life harder for me. That is JESUS. He can do what He wants, when He wants and to sinners like me, help when we <u>call His name.</u>

Psalm 140:5 "The arrogant have hidden a snare for me, they have spread out the cords of their net and have set traps for me along my path." Psalm 57:6 "They spread a net for me feet – I was bowed in distress. They dug a pit in my path – but they have fallen into it themselves."

This was true what my LORD GOD JESUS said to me, both neighbors efforts and time fell to dust and would not accept JESUS' Will. They both continued their hearings, and being of this world and not allowing JESUS' Will be done, rather they both listened to the whispers of lucifer the devil.

JESUS told me in advance they would fall to their own net. I have strong faith in JESUS. They are mad at JESUS and not me, as I choose to take His path and not the long path to His will being done.

JESUS is power and beyond our understanding, but I do hear JESUS clearly then and now. There is NOTHING beyond the power of GOD. Evil will be destroyed. Evil will witness their fate soon. Do you hear evil men of this world? Repent and Believe what JESUS has said. There is no time to wait. You will never survive without JESUS.

Different standards exist even among Christians. I mention this because of the busy body troubles that the devil escalates into mounds of dung simply by whispering into their ears repeatedly for years.

The Ten Commandments neighbor's judgments, her condemning others has cost her three failed marriages. The power steering is broken again, I wondered if I should text my neighbor across the street as to why my car is hard to control, but I wont.

If she gets angry again it will be with JESUS again, cause it was JESUS who drove my car out of the snow over the "right of way" she got mad over. I tried, but couldn't drive the car, so I said, "You do it JESUS, I cannot drive the car out of my driveway, I am stuck." JESUS did, so my Christian neighbor was upset with JESUS.

The demons knew it was JESUS who drove my car and schemed to use my Christian neighbor to condemn me. Hypocrisy and Condemnation is thick. [40]"The LORD says, these people come near to me with their mouth and honor me with their lips, but their hearts are far from me. Their worship of me is made up only of rules taught by men." John the Baptist said to hypocritical neighbors, [41] "produce fruits worthy of repentance."

She spoke of this "Patti" whom demons use to torment me, even threw snow and dirt into my face with a shovel. She is a Jehovah Witness and a neighbor too. She is filled with hate and bitterness.

---

[40] Isaiah 29:13; Matthew 15:8-9

[41] Luke 3:8

I pray for [42] her a lot even before knowing what their beliefs are. She wants people to think she is a widow, but this old gal has been married three separate times and each one last a year with her filing for divorce. Father, in Your name JESUS I pray You open her eyes to the truth about You, and Holy Spirit. I pray the chains of hate and evil be broken and replace with love. I pray repentance and belief in You JESUS as the divine Son of GOD. Amen. Speaking of evil and mean neighbors, hypocrisy is what runs our government until President Trump appeared and placed JESUS first.

JESUS no longer sees his sins and Christians don't care about his [43] womanizing and other sins of the past. We have all sinned. Our government on all levels in every state in the USA is the worst in hypocrisy and condemnation. JESUS called hypocrites [44] "wolves in sheep's clothing," "whitewashed tombs," "snakes," and "brood of vipers."

How can you love your brothers, your neighbors and this country if with luciferian hypocrisy? It is all a façade with these government officials and all this fake news from all news outlets except a righteous few like Fox and Newsmax and those they endorse.

[45] Do you love GOD? Do you want to know the truth about GOD? If you die are you going to His Kingdom? Do you want to know how to avoid Hell?

[46] " Will not the ministry of the Holy Spirit have even more glory?" My faith in JESUS our LORD GOD is so strong nothing of creation can harm me. My trust in JESUS surpasses all understanding. JESUS is my destiny.

---

[42] Matthew 5:45

[43] Matthew 6:15

[44] Matthew 7:15; Matthew 23:27; Matthew 23:33

[45] 1 John 2:9; Romans 12:9

[46] Matthew 23:5; 2Corinthians 3:8

I recently was bit by a brown recluse spider on my right knee. JESUS said, "Trust in ME." I told my husband and showed everyone the bite. I told JESUS that I trusted Him. Nothing happened to me from the poisonous bite. It bruised, and JESUS did allow me to taste the fowl venom of the spider in my saliva for three days. It tasted wrenched. I had no repercussions from that bite and know from JESUS that [47] neither vipers nor any crawling venomous creatures can harm me.

[48]"I have given you authority to trample on snakes and scorpions and to overcome all the power of the enemy, nothing will harm you." I stepped on a scorpion in Arizona and not affected by the poison in that scorpion.

Roseanne Barr is another who sees the truth of this world and has repented. Father, In Your Name JESUS I pray she removes all other idols from her life and only worships You JESUS. Amen.

Hypocrisy is why her show was cancelled. Hypocrisy, Hypocrisy, and Hypocrisy is the foundation with ABC and all luciferian networks that speak not of our LORD GOD JESUS openly. It is true about ambien causing ill effects to where flesh does irreversible unthinkable actions, of which Roseanne repented and asked forgiveness. Tim Allen (also went to prison) is a good soul and salvation his, as a son of GOD. He too was in prison.

---

[47] Mark 16:18

[48] Luke 10:19

"Paul of Tarsus" is my Great, Great, Great (etc.) Uncle. Paul is from the tribe of Benjamin. Funny, I drive a $300.00 white Ford Taurus that JESUS got for me right out of prison. Call me Yvonne who drives a Taurus. Benjamin, Joseph's brother and Rachael's youngest son is my Great, Great, Great (etc.) Grandfather. Paul had Roman credentials and I do too. I have Roman credentials. Paul was the chief sinner of sinners. I too am a chief sinner and broken all the Ten Commandments.

The Tribe of Judah and the Tribe of Benjamin are my Tribe, Me. JESUS said not to "get caught up in my genealogy." I have am Tribe of Benjamin, African, Native American (Apache, etc...), Hebrew, British, Irish, Iberian, Italian, Spain, French, German, Sardinian, European, Balkan, Ashkenazi Jewish (like Albert Einstein) I truly am a creation of GOD.

I was a corrupted person with a heart. I used my beauty to a certain point, and then guilt was felt. My conscious would set in. Although Grace saves us, the Ten Commandment still holds to the hearts of all.
JESUS CHRIST did not do away with the Ten Commandments. [49]"Do not think that I have come to abolish the Law (Ten Commandments) or the Prophets; I have not come to abolish them but to fulfill them. For truly I tell you, until heaven and earth disappear, not the smallest letter, not the least stroke of
a pen, will by any means disappear from the Law until everything is accomplished."

The devil, satan (lucifer) who's throne was in Pergamos and still may be (Roman Catholic), wants GOD'S children to think Grace did away with the Law, but fact and truth is the Ten Commandments are written in your heart when you are born-again (saved). JESUS sums the Ten Commandments with,

---

[49] Matthew 5:17-18

[50]"Thou shall love the LORD thy GOD with all thy heart, and with all thy soul, and with all they mind. This is the first and great commandment. And the second is like unto it, Thou shall love thy neighbor as thyself. On these two commandments hang all the law and the prophets." If you obey these two commands then you don't want to kill, steal, etc.

I had several abortions for vain reasons. I was a horrible person who thought the only good from pregnancy was the initial weight lost. I chose to live immorally with no thought of my destiny. My ignorance at the time was thinking life began after birth and not during conception. The last abortion I had I remember thinking to myself, I hope GOD does not acknowledge it. That perhaps it would be overlooked. That was back in 1990. We are born sinners. Repent from self-righteousness.

I spoke earlier about aborting a child in my belly and thinking GOD won't know my heart and when I am before Him, perhaps my aborting this child without telling anyone (in darkness), will be seen by no one, not even GOD. I was demonically wrong.

I sinned a lot thinking if no one saw or caught me sinning, then GOD would not notice. Wrong. How stupid of thinking that I was. GOD sees all and is everywhere at all times.

I have learned in faith, "For everyone practicing evil hates the light and does not come to the light lest his deeds should be expose. But he who does the truth comes to the light, that his deeds may clearly be seen, that they have been done in GOD."

---

[50] Mark 12:30-31; Matthew 22:36-40; Luke 10:27

If you can't live in the light, if your actions are not goodness, then you are being controlled by devils. Do acts of goodness for GOD to see. Don't believe there is a force of nature that energizes this world. GOD is the energy and power.

GOD gives you rest from all the troubles of this world. Consent to be loved and rest on the stronger shoulder's of our LORD, JESUS. Receive the gift of righteousness in JESUS. My neighbor with a good heart (Ten Commandment posted on her house/church), who has a church across my home, came over and told me a gentleman was going to be a speaker that day. I cooked something and as I opened the door I fell to my knees and told the whole congregation that I had several abortions tearfully twice over. Hal, the speaker said JESUS has already forgiven me.

I did not know what was happening to me, but I felt a mourning of some sort. I experienced an earthly death. I went through a phase of needing to tell my fellow Christians, I had abortions. I recalled I John 1:9, and wanted to apply my need to obey the Lord our GOD. Day's prior I told GOD I wanted to state the abortions aloud. GOD knows my heart and had me profess what weighed on me to the President of Pro Life for Montana. I did not know he was, but GOD knew I wanted to tell my mistake to people who would hear me. GOD being all was showing Hal some things too. I think it had to do with his mission in Life for GOD.

When saved, born again, all sins are removed. The only authority we have is the word of GOD. The Gospel of the Kingdom of GOD (Holy Bible) speaks out all you need to know. Know what the LORD JESUS has to say by reading the gospel.

I was hesitant knowing in the back of my mind that my life would change. It was not the change I thought it would be. It is fulfillment. True life is fulfillment. Be associated with JESUS and not all this world has to offer.

The Body of CHRIST JESUS will contain all believers, all aborted children, all Old Testament saints and dead children who were not at the age of accountability. GOD commanded us not to choose to eat from the "tree of knowledge of good and evil, but to eat from the "Tree of Life."

Pro-choice people are choosing the route, the destiny to hell, the eternal "Lake of Fire" abode. The joke is on them when they see all the aborted children in the Kingdom of GOD while being cast into the "Lake of Fire" with satan, the demons and all evil that ever existed…forever and ever, pain that never ceases, ever. Adam is the first man GOD created. GOD gave Adam the reign of the earth. Adam named all the animals of the earth. GOD said to Adam do not eat from that tree and the day you do you will die. Believe Adam was conned by the devil, ate from that tree, and was cut off from GOD.

Listen up all you people who don't understand GOD. Do you want to know the truth about life after death and the only two destinies willfully chosen by you right now while you still have a chance to repent and believe? That is the message I am conveying for JESUS. Repent and believe in JESUS. Repent and believe in JESUS. Repent and believe in JESUS. Again, do you not want to know the Truth that GODISJESUSLIVES? JESUS does not want to be separated from you, but it is your choice.

You are a spirit that can never die, so do you want heaven or hell? Repentance is changing your mind towards GOD. Repentance is truly feeling remorse and sincere regret towards (in the direction of) GOD. GOD defines us as JESUS. As JESUS is so are we when we rest in Him. Be transformed by beholding JESUS, by the Spirit of JESUS we are transformed. We become the righteousness of GOD.

The Gospel of JESUS is the Gospel of Grace. Once you believe in JESUS you become justified, made righteous from all things that could not be justified by the Ten Commandments. Once saved by Grace of GOD, you realize there is but one living GOD. No more premeditated evil scenarios leading me to lie, steal, or commit adultery. You love GOD above all things and you love your neighbor, others as you love yourself.

You can be saved while a sinner. Of course not intentional sinning…You get saved to better yourself. Take the love of JESUS and keep it by giving it to others, your neighbor.

For those of you who believe that JESUS is just a prophet, He is much more. JESUS himself revealed to us that He is the Son of GOD and GOD in the flesh. Turn away from just believing He was only a prophet. Repent of the unbelief. We cannot know all our sins as creatures of GOD until GOD opens our mind and reveals how wretched we are, how pure loving GOD is. Unbelievers, change your mind about JESUS. JESUS was sent by GOD, "GOD so loved us that he gave us His only begotten Son that whosoever believes in JESUS will have everlasting life." How much our Creator, our GOD loves us that He would adopt us. GOD is for us. GOD wants to bless us. GOD helps walk away from pornography, adultery, murdering, stealing, lying or whatever is binding you to not be morally upright. Even with all those faults, you can be saved. Even if you backslide, you will never lose your position in the Kingdom of GOD once saved, truly saved.

Repent and consent to allow JESUS to love you, that is GOD. Sincere regret, sincere remorse and genuinely turning to GOD and faith in JESUS will save you. Consent to be carried by JESUS. Consent to rest in JESUS. Allow yourself to be carried, resting in JESUS and rejoicing in the power of GOD.

JESUS prayed to His Father GOD, desiring that we whom He gave to JESUS His Son may be with JESUS, [51]"where I Am, that they may behold My glory which You have given Me; for You loved Me before the foundation of the world." Long before this world, long before all that is in this world and long before us all, was CHRIST. All things were created by, CHRIST JESUS. It is a fact that GOD the Father loved CHRIST before the foundations of the world. Again I repeat, "For GOD so loved the world that He gave His only begotten Son, that whoever believes in Him should not perish but have everlasting life."

Does not matter how young or old you are, choose life eternal. GOD so loved the world, not just the Jews, all persons, all sinners. GOD gave His only Son CHRIST to die on the cross for our sins.

JESUS is CHRIST whom GOD the Father sent as a baby boy. That baby boy is JESUS. JESUS' death was not a murder; to say that JESUS was murdered, is to say GOD is a murderer. GOD sent JESUS to die for us, in our place. There was no other way to save us from death eternal. The Son of GOD, CHRIST was sent to take a physical body and die on the cross. GOD is righteous and loves us beyond comprehension that He would send His son, CHRIST JESUS to die for our past, present and future sins.

JESUS' death was planned by, GOD and CHRIST. JESUS was not murdered. JESUS freely gave himself to die on the cross. No one can take the life of JESUS. No one could have saved himself from the sins of this world. It took JESUS to save us. There was no other way for us to be saved. Believe in JESUS and be saved.

Choose life eternal and not perishing into utter darkness with all evil, in eternal suffering. Narrow is the way to everlasting life of love, only through JESUS. Wide is the

---

[51] John 17:24

path to destruction, through non-belief of JESUS.[52]"Make every effort to enter through the narrow door, because many, I tell you, will try to enter and will not be able to." Choose the Kingdom of GOD. Give your life to JESUS. Believe in JESUS, GOD'S purpose for sending our Lord CHRIST JESUS, [53]"that the world through Him might be saved."
GODISJESUSLIVES.

JESUS is exalted. No person or creation is higher than our GOD is, JESUS is. GOD the Father, [54]"highly exalted Him and given Him the name which is above every name." "That at the name of JESUS every knee should bow, of things in heaven and in earth, and things under the earth." Wow! "And that every tongue should confess that JESUS CHRIST is Lord." Receive JESUS. Do not wait until it is too late. Do not let the last moment in the presence of JESUS be in regret. Hell is real and is everlasting torment. I know JESUS. He is real and is GOD the Son. He is precious. He is my GOD, my Father, my Savior, and my Lord. There is power in the name, JESUS. We do all things in the name of JESUS. We pray in the name of JESUS to GOD the Father. Apart from JESUS, we have no standing before Almighty GOD. JESUS intercedes for us as the Son of GOD.

JESUS is our only access to GOD Almighty, His Father. Know JESUS and let him represent you before GOD Almighty. Only in JESUS, can we find and live eternally with GOD. Pray in the name of JESUS to GOD. JESUS saves. Only JESUS saves and can forgives sins. Be saved. [55]"Nor is there salvation in any other, for there is no other name under heaven given among men by which we must we saved."

---

[52] Luke 13:24

[53] John 3:17

[54] Philippians 2:9-11

[55] Acts 4:12-14

IN THE NAME OF JESUS, you can command evil to depart from you. Have faith and let JESUS save you. JESUS is the Savior of the world. CHRIST JESUS has come to, [56]"seek and to save that which was lost." JESUS said if you have seen me, you have seen the Father. Trust in JESUS.
Rejecting JESUS is eternal doom. Do not reject the truth GOD has told us. I witness JESUS is alive and is our Savior. I tell you truth. Do not reject salvation. Rejecting the gospel is rejecting GOD. [57]That is the only unforgivable sin; blaspheme of the Holy Spirit of GOD. Not believing in JESUS will send you straight to eternal suffering. The sin debt has been paid by CHRIST JESUS for the first and last time, believe it and live eternal in the Kingdom of GOD.

[58] "Enter by the narrow gate; for wide is the gate and broad is the way that leads to destruction, and there are many who go in by it. Because narrow is the gate and difficult is the way which leads to life, and there are few who find it." Choose life! Choose life!!! All you people who are pro choice and help ignorant woman and girls abort GOD'S children heed what JESUS says or you will suffer eternal damnation while I play with all those aborted children in the Kingdom of GOD.

Find JESUS and believe in JESUS, which is the path to eternal life. Do not be separated from your loved ones by not believing in the resurrection of JESUS as the Son of GOD. Have a relationship with JESUS. GOD desires all be saved. JESUS is our redeemer. The devil takes advantage if men's sin. JESUS did not pay the devil for our sins, but paid GOD the Father.

---

[56] Luke 19:10

[57] Mark 3:28-30

[58] Matthew 7:15

The devil, satan and his demons are created by GOD with no power over us believers. JESUS is the Grace of the Holy GOD who paid GOD the Father for His justice, redeeming our inheritance. It was not a debt of the devil. The devil or his demons have no power over JESUS or us believers. The devil uses half-truths and trickery, and is able to give the appearance of miracles. The devil will even use the Holy Bible against you, tricking you to believe things, and using GOD'S name to coerce you. The devil, all fallen evil angels and [59] demons know JESUS, the divine Son of GOD. lucifer and his demons know our Lord JESUS to be their Creator, their GOD. The evil angles know their time on earth is coming to an abrupt end. Into the "Lake of Fire" prepared for them and their followers, luciferians.

The devil and his demons will always take advantage of you if you let that evil unholy angelic spirit. Evil has no power over GOD'S people. Free yourself and walk in the redemption of CHRIST JESUS. Remember JESUS is Grace. It took the death of JESUS CHRIST to defeat death and to save us by Grace.

There is power given us by JESUS. There is power in the name of JESUS. Use it faithfully. Do not grieve the Holy Spirit of GOD. Paul says by the words of JESUS told to him, "And do not grieve the Holy Spirit of GOD, by whom you were sealed for the day of redemption. Let all bitterness, wrath, anger, clamor, and evil speaking be put away from you, with all malice. And be kind to one another, tenderhearted, forgiving one another, even as GOD in CHRIST forgave you." The forgiveness of GOD in CHRIST is the Grace of GOD. We have been saved from death by JESUS' death on the cross.

---

[59] Matthew 8:29-30

We are no longer under the curse, under the law, but saved by Grace. The New Testament is all about the Grace of GOD. You are a "new creation" in CHRIST when saved. "Therefore, as the elect of GOD, holy and beloved, put on tender mercies, kindness, humility, meekness, longsuffering; bearing with one another, and forgiving one another, if anyone has a complaint against another, even as CHRIST forgave you, so you also must do. But above all things put on love, which is the bond of perfection. And let the peace of GOD rule in your hearts, to which you were called in one body; and be thankful."

"Set your mind on things above, not on things on the earth." You see, under the law, we forgave one another in order to be forgiven, but under Grace, we forgive because we have already been forgiven. Some people go strictly by the words in red in the New Testament, which are truth and before JESUS was glorified. Meditate in knowing truth.

4

DO NOT BELIEVE EVIL SPIRIRTS PRETENTDING TO BE HOLY ANGELIC SPIRITS

It is written in the Gospel, the Holy Bible, "Beloved, do not believe every spirit, but test the spirits to see whether they are from GOD; because many false prophets have gone into the world. How you know if they have the Spirit of GOD: If a person claiming to be a prophet acknowledges (confesses) that JESUS CHRIST has come in the flesh (a real body) is from the Spirit of GOD; but if someone claims to be a prophet and does not acknowledge the truth about JESUS, that person is not from GOD.

Such a person has a spirit of the antichrist, which you heard is coming into the world and indeed already here." Old testament scriptures foretold this fact, this truth. America is no better than the Israelites who are waiting for GOD messiah Son to arrive.

Every person in this country should know that we are in the end time, approaching the very coming of CHRIST JESUS. The tribulation, the suffering is forthcoming. The world government and appearance of the anti Christ is near future. Most people in these 50 states do not even know how near the end times. Most people choose to remain ignorant. You do not have to be ignorant of these truths.

JESUS is King of Heaven and has Earth, of all. Israel did not obtain the truth that nation looked for and remains spiritually blind. You do not have to be without knowledge of truth. JESUS is Truth. GOD revealed to an election of Jews, JESUS is His Son, by Faith, they see. Jews will remain spiritual blind until the fullness of the Gentiles (anyone who is not Jewish), until the last Gentile has been told of JESUS CHRIST and given his life over to JESUS-born again.

The terror of tribulation is both physical and mental. It will test your ability to keep sanity. You do not want to be here for the tribulation which is soon here. Choose eternal life with JESUS. GODISJESUSLIVES.

Do not choose eternal life in utter darkness where you shall suffer forever and ever eternal. Divorce yourself from this world. Be in the world and not of the world. Horror is on the Earth. The tribulation will be the final 7 years and never has there been or ever again, the horror that is upon this earth. We are approaching the final years here on earth. Look around.

See all the evilness, wickedness we humans are practices upon one another. Unspeakable torture this sinful world. All areas of this world is fallen to lucifer, the created fallen angel satan, the deceiver. The wrath of GOD is going to be poured out on those that chose evil satan. In all of GOD dealing with the human race, the nation of Israel is at the center of it all.

The deceiver, satan hates what GOD loves. GOD loves the nation of Israel. The world does not want to believe that one little nation of a few million people is at the core of GODS plan. Billions of people surround Israel. Corruption will not inherit corruption. The tribulation will be cataclysmic around the world.

JESUS is most high. JESUS is Lord. JESUS is GOD. GOD is GOD the Father, GOD the Son and GOD the Holy Spirit. We were created with the mind, the body, and soul. That too is three in one. GOD breathed life into us giving each one of us a spirit eternal. With all the horrible evil acts by us, GOD will no longer allow His created to defile His creations. His land is filled with abominations. He gave us His land to use and we have defiled it with spilled blood, immoral acts.

Be ashamed of the committed abominations. Blush for the immortal acts. GOD is Grace. He freely gives us unmerited favor once we ask for it. Ask for it. Do not choose satan. Do not choose utter darkness after death.

See how GOD gave the Israelis a country of their own as an inheritance. They made that land an abomination before GRACE had entered. GOD became man, and JESUS defeated death. Know that JESUS is CHRIST. I was a horrible example of a person years ago. It was not until I put JESUS first, my eyes opened. I aced so many life problems from probably lifetime incarceration to being alienated by all, friends and family included.

Lust ruled my life. I could go on and on about my life trials, but salvation, life eternal is all about JESUS. JESUS wants all to be saved from eternal damnation. All things are held together by, JESUS. I said before, I was created to be a child of GOD and born to give testimony that GODISJESUSLIVES.

JESUS left heavens glory to save us all when JESUS bore the torture, the scourging of His back and by His [60]bloody stripes; we are healed and saved from our sins. In everyday problems, JESUS would talk me through it. I asked and received. No one can speak to GOD, but the Son of GOD, JESUS.

My husband will not watch Mel Gibson's great depiction movie, "The Passion of the CHRIST" because it sadden him to see reality of the scourging JESUS took for us, but in reality the beating of His flesh left Him disfigured to the point that only His bones showed. The people JESUS created beat Him so bad, all you saw was flesh hanging and visible bones hanging on the cross.

[61]"No one tales my life away from me. I sacrifice it voluntarily. For I have the authority to lay it down when I want to and also to take it up again. For this is what my Father has commanded."

---

[60] Isaiah 53:5

[61] John 10:18

I know JESUS inspired Mel, a JESUS boy, to direct this great movie. I hear there is a sequel to this movie and I look forward to it. Father, in Your name JESUS I pray gracious blessings upon Your son Mel, his family and all those he loves and prays for. Amen.

Shout Grace to all your problems. Only GOD can remove all your problems, no man can. Pray loud to Lord JESUS for Grace into all situations whether prior to or after your actions. Have Faith that Lord JESUS handles every aspect of your life. When you are down and out, put your head in the Holy Scriptures of GOD, the Holy Bible (Gospel).

The devil wants you to fall and define yourself as the sinner we are. The devil and his followers are always trying to convince us to be of this world. To think we are doomed and useless. Not to be forgiving or loving to others is what wants. If GOD allowed us to see the invisible, we would see all the Holy Angels and fallen angels (unclean spirits) around us. It is what we do not see that is real.

JESUS is your sanctification. He is the only way to eternal life. The other way is utter eternal darkness. You have no other choice as a creature of GOD created by, and through JESUS CHRIST. Start thinking, believing and speaking the faith of JESUS. Save yourself. All you peoples, both Old Testament Jews and non-Jews.

Faith in JESUS overcomes the world. When you exercise faith in JESUS, you overcome lucifer the devil, fallen angels the demons, and their followers in the flesh. GOD gives you free will to choose your destiny, but you only have 2 choices.

Some people chose evil, and evil is their destiny where there will be eternal torment. Forever and ever, they will be aware of their choosing. Join me and other JESUS girls and boys where we are children of GOD. Forever and ever, we will be in love, joy and utopia.

No human can imagine or can describe the Kingdom of GOD. Trust in JESUS. He is our righteousness. JESUS' death on the cross, justified us to be morally right in GODS eyes. Good works for others does not justify us. Speak aloud your faith in JESUS and it will be in your heart.

When you are fearful, speak that GOD gave you the power of love and of a sound mind. JESUS is power. Our love for GOD gives us the same power by faith though JESUS. Say aloud, "I can do all things through JESUS CHRIST who strengthen me."

The Holy Bible, the word of JESUS says, "The word is near you, in your mouth and in your heart". First your mouth, followed by your heart. The devil does not want you to learn to speak it first. The devil wants you to act holy first. It is not how we think, but how JESUS has told us.

I speak from personal experience. JESUS showed me things. JESUS led the way. JESUS told me things before I ever read the Holy Bible. It was in 2009 that I asked myself what was the most important book in the world. I was recovering from a surgery and had down time. Looking across and over to the wall, I laid there, I saw stacks of Holy Bibles and knew my answer. I read the book of Job and cried for 2 weeks.

I never saw a Holy Bible other than in the Church. The first book in the bible I read was the "Book of Job. I cried for two weeks. I have been studying the Holy Bible for 9 years and I meditate in the Word of GOD everyday for hours, which is normal for me.

Paul's words are from the Glorified CHRIST JESUS. After the death of JESUS, all people could be saved whether Jew or not. You are saved in CHRIST JESUS. Being saved by CHRIST JESUS is a gift He freely offers. Take the gift of salvation by confessing with your mouth that JESUS is Lord. That He gave His life on the cross for the remission of all sins of the world.

Believe in your heart that GOD raised Him from the dead. Say JESUS, I believe you are the Son of GOD. I believe You are GOD in the flesh sent by GOD the Father. I believe You gave your life freely and laid it down at the cross where You where crucified for our sins. You took our place of judgment and died for the remission of my sins. You took my judgment upon yourself. I believe JESUS is my Lord and Savior and my GOD. I believe JESUS rose again in fulfillment of the Holy Scriptures. I believe JESUS is resurrected and is seated at the right hand of our Heavenly Father GOD. I believe JESUS will come again. JESUS I believe, "For GOD so loved the world that He gave His only begotten Son (JESUS) that whosoever believes in Him shall not parish but have everlasting life." Amen. This is Grace. Say these words to GOD, let JESUS enter you and have willfully chosen eternal life with GOD. Truth is, "For GOD did not send His Son (JESUS) into the world to condemn the world, but that the world through Him might be saved. He who believes in Him is not condemned, but he who does not believe is condemned already, because he has not believed in the name of the only begotten Son of GOD." You are secure in CHRIST JESUS.

JESUS did not intend us to be our own democratic organization. All nations and empires, everyone will fall to JESUS who is our Creator. It will be too late if you die and have not accepted that JESUS is GOD the Son. It will be too late if you wait to see JESUS coming through the clouds to save us from the anti CHRIST during these end times. Don't risk being separated from those you love and willfully choosing not to believe, ending up in hell eternal, where you will remember not choosing life eternal in the Kingdom of GOD with all His Glory.

You can have a personal relationship with GOD. You need no interceders, but the Holy Spirit of GOD. Call on JESUS. GOD wants to have a relationship with you, personally. It occurred to me several years ago that all the emotions we feel GOD has and gave us a few of those feelings. It hurt my heart to know we His creatures have hurt His heart. We are made in the image of GOD. Unbelievers' won't be able to make a deal when he sees JESUS coming through the clouds. We are not to judge, but we are to hate sin.

So many times GOD has made our lives less stressful and encouraging. I have always believed in JESUS, but was not born again, saved until my 40's. GOD takes a single happening and able to touch the lives of billions with the single gesture of love. Remember that man invented religions. Christianity is not a religion; it is spirituality of the Kingdom of GOD. GODISJESUSLIVES.

Choose everlasting life and be saved, born again in the spirit of GOD. JESUS is GOD and created us. JESUS died for our sins and did not let all of us to parish and enter hell everlasting. We now have a choice to believe in JESUS by faith and choose everlasting life in the Kingdom of GOD, Heaven.

GOD had the choice of letting us all parish and created a new creation, but love is in His heart. We are made in the image of GOD. Creation for GOD is speaking a word from His mouth, just like when He created this world, GOD said, "Let there be Light" and there was light. GOD is speaking to His Son, JESUS and to His Holy Spirit. JESUS chose to die on the cross and bleed (blood) to buy us back from death and hell. None of His creations could have saved us from hell. There is no sin in JESUS or in His flesh.

GOD is Holy. Holy is sacred and divine. GOD hallowed (sanctified: set aside and declared holy: consecrated and blessed) His name. Hallowed means Holy, sacred and blessed.

GOD also hallowed the seventh day, Saturday. That is the day GOD rested from creating this world. GOD commanded us to keep Holy and rest. Saturday is the day JESUS sanctified Israel. "I the Lord do sanctify Israel." "Lord GOD made; Lord GOD took; Lord GOD commanded; Lord GOD said; Lord GOD formed; Lord GOD walked; Lord GOD called..." "They shall know; They shall know; They shall know..." I AM GOD." GOD has said many time, "I will..." If the law is written in your heart (which it is) when saved by Grace, then that included all Ten Commandments. These are the laws written in our hearts when born again and saved by Grace and becoming a JESUS girl or JESUS boy. Sunday is for Church to worship GOD.

[62]Saturday is the day GOD sanctified in Genesis 2:3 and set aside for us to keep and rest. For people like pastors and Grace gospel preachers to say that Saturday rest is just for Jews is the same as saying the Ten Commandments is just for Jews and not saved believers in JESUS. I rest on Saturdays because Saturday Made Holy By GOD. I am not a Seventh Day Adventist or Seventh Day Baptist, but I try more and more to keep Saturday (Sabbath), a Holy day of rest at home with family, dedicated to GOD. If you gas up load the family and drive your vehicle to a church, is that work, yes to me. Jared and Ivanka do it right.

If the fourth Commandment by GOD is just for the Jews, then all other nine Commandments including Do not murder, Obey your mother and father, Do not steal, Do not commit adultery, Have no other gods before me, etc., only apply to Jews and written in the hearts of (Messianic JESUS believing Jews)? Don't be stupid, of course Saturday Holy rest applies to all children of GOD. Quit justifying a lie by ignoring the truth.

---

[62] Genesis 2:3

We are not under the law, Ten Commandments written in the heart once you become born again, but you are to obey the law. We cannot uphold the law because are flesh is evil and only JESUS was perfect. That is where Grace saves us. We are under Grace, but the two go hand in hand and easy to understand the wisdom of what I am saying when you are born-again. "Have you not known? Have you not heard?

The everlasting GOD, the Lord, the Creator of the ends of the earth, neither faints nor is weary. His understanding, His ways is unknowable. He gives power to the weak, and to those who have no might He increases strength." Nothing can separate us from the love of GOD. JESUS died to sin once and for all people. JESUS was never under the power of sin or guilt, but we were once and never again. JESUS bore our punishment. Do not let any one tell you differently. JESUS died for us, on that cross. JESUS bore our judgments. There is no longer condemnation. We have been healed.

JESUS said, "Do not think that I have come to do away with or undo the Law, or the prophets; I have come not to do away with or undo, but to complete and fulfill them." JESUS fulfilled all the laws. JESUS also said, "For truly, I tell you, until the sky and earth pass away, not one smallest letter nor one little hook [identifying Hebrew letters which look like little hooks] will pass from the Law until all things have been accomplished [foreshadow: future event."

JESUS did not abolish the Law, the Ten Commandments; this was made clear during JESUS' "Sermon on the Mount." Know that we will worship JESUS in His Kingdom. JESUS did do away with the hundreds of law Moses wrote for the Jews, but not the Ten Commandments GOD gave to Moses to all of us creatures of His.

Spiritual baptism is the only baptism you must have. Not water baptism, but Spiritual baptism. "For by one Spirit (Holy Spirit) are we all baptized into one body." If you are a Jehovah Witness you better pay attention to what JESUS say the Holy Spirit. Many Jehovah Witness are doomed for not understanding GOD the Father, GOD the Son and GOD the Holy Spirit. Do Jehovah Witnesses really think that their paradise book from the Dead Sea Scroll does not join JESUS' death on the cross? You Old Testament worshippers better understand the New Testament (Gospel of Grace); they go hand in hand. The Gospel of Grace is what saves you from the Lake of Fire eternal. You better ask JESUS.

GOD is almighty and place the Holy Bible in your hand. Read it and save yourself with the free will to choose eternal life in JESUS. Holy Spirit is a person. He is GOD the Spirit. If you do not have the Holy Spirit baptism, not water, you will not see GOD'S Glory. This is the only true baptism everybody better have or you are not going to be in GOD'S Glory, if you have this baptism then your name is written in the "Lamb's Book of Life" with mine and others saved by the Spiritual baptism. Wake up you non-believer and fake Christians.

The Body of CHRIST is humongous. Those in CHRIST will rule and reign with CHRIST JESUS. We will be able to go throughout the heavenly sphere. It is unspeakable joy. The only organization that shall remain is the body of CHRIST eternal. Those in the body of CHRIST will be those redeemed, many members of us saints in the most High GOD, JESUS. Amen. We are called out of darkness and into the body of Christ outlasting even heaven and earth. We who believe in JESUS will be church in His body.

GOD is, merciful. He has called us to salvation. Those who hear will be saved. Be a believer and be redeemed. Almost believing in JESUS does not redeem you. Do not prefer the darkness. Do not say no to eternal life. Be repenting by changing your darkness to light. Truth is what I write for GODISJESUSLIVES. Amen.

GOD will not violate your free choice of choosing eternal joy or eternal hell and suffering. It is your choice, but how long do you have to choose. You could die right now. This world is getting worse and shall continue to get worse. GOD has revealed what I write to us all. The blessings in my life and others have gotten greater and greater. GOD always has words for those who listen. Listen now. Listen to the LORD who speaks directly to you. Only GOD can help you with complaining spirits who are attacking your mind. Only GOD can help you with your worried heart that the spirits of worry continues to tell your mind. Only GOD can help you with that critical evil spirit who critiques all you do at all times.

All the bad things in life only JESUS can help you overcome. JESUS is the weapon. JESUS is the amour. JESUS is the wisdom. JESUS holds the equipment to defeat those problems, not you but JESUS. You and me, we are dirt, but JESUS is what keeps our spirit alive eternal.

The earth shall continue to get worse, so save your spirit and Repent by consenting to allow JESUS to love you, that is repentance to GOD. Grace and Truth came through JESUS. The Truth will set you free. Listen to the Word of GOD. Choose life eternal in the Kingdom of GOD. Grace is the Truth that will set you free, free to all who take it. GOD said HE would be merciful to our unrighteousness and your sins, I will remember no more. GOD spoke of Grace in the Gospel with the prophet Jeremiah in the Old Testament and again in the New Testament. JESUS saved us from eternal damnation, with Grace.

Grace saves us. Be thankful that you have little time to be saved. Again, save yourself by saying these words and truly by faith accepting JESUS as the Son of GOD.

Pray, JESUS I believe you are the Son of GOD. I believe You are GOD in the flesh sent by GOD the Father. I believe You gave your life freely and laid it down at the cross where You where crucified for our sins. You JESUS took our place of judgment and died for the remission of my sins and took my judgment upon yourself. I believe JESUS is my LORD and Savior and my GOD. I believe JESUS rose again in fulfillment of the Holy Scriptures. I believe JESUS is resurrected and is seated at the right hand of our Heavenly Father GOD.

I believe JESUS will come again. JESUS I believe, "For GOD so loved the world that He gave His only begotten Son (JESUS) that whosoever believes in Him shall not parish but have everlasting life." Amen.

Again, I tell you, this is Grace. If you have said the above prayer/words to GOD then you have chosen to let JESUS enter you and have willfully chosen eternal life with GOD. Throughout the book JESUS has me repeating the abovementioned prayer to salvation.

This is the message from JESUS, **repent** by sinning no more and **believe** in Him as the Son of GOD. GODISJESUSLIVES.

We are at the end of time here on Earth, in the flesh. JESUS CHRIST is coming the moment the body of CHRIST is complete. When the last Gentile or Jew is saved, then CHRIST JESUS will come for the church. I rest in the body of CHRIST.

GODISJESUSLIVES

5

JOSEPH PRINCE GOSPEL OF GRACE JESUS BOYS AND GIRLS

You want a true understanding of JESUS, go watch or read what Joseph Prince has to say. He is the most wise, knowledgeable and used servant of GOD. JESUS uses him to teach with power and Grace. There exist no other man on earth who has complete understanding of the Gospel of Grace. Second would be Robert Morris. No one will be misled by these two Grace teachers, nobody. JESUS led me to Joseph Prince and Les Feldick (for believers) to meditate on their knowledge and teachings for years (almost a decade just studying their teachings).

There are times as now where for months I hear and learn the same message over and over again, 24/7 from these two sons of GOD. Amazing is what JESUS has revealed to Joseph Prince. Hear, watch and hear what JESUS has revealed to Joseph Prince. JESUS Himself told me to let everyone know what a mighty man of GOD Joseph is. How blessed Singapore, New Creation Church is to have JESUS place Joseph with them.

JESUS told me Joseph is equal to my great uncle Paul of Tarsus, in the latter times with regards to the Gospel of Grace, JESUS speaks to Joseph.

Joseph Prince is the most important man in the world (not the Pope) since Billy Graham's death according to JESUS. Wendy, Jessica, Justin, your husband, your Dad has been a man like King David, after GOD'S heart. Most Popes have been evil, only a few are righteous, only GOD knows.

Joseph Prince has been speaking to GOD his entire life. JESUS has groomed him for the latter days for us. Be saved and enter the Kingdom of GOD, listen to the Gospel of Grace that Joseph teacher's so easily. Be thankful we have Joseph with us on earth. Singapore, New Creation Church, how blessed you are. JESUS has told me much about Joseph being chosen by Him, a loyal son of His. Amen.

The devil will fight your entering with labor of annoyances, anger, frustration, by throwing thoughts to you that you need to do this or that. Attend to all matters from an attitude of rest, rather than worry and urgency.

My husband was leaving every Monday morning at 4 am to go to work in a different town. He was gone for four days every week. He left again and immediately I was confronted by 20 more or less demons. They each tried to enter my body through my head/mind. While sleeping, I said "JESUS" repeatedly. This is not the first time demons were rebuked in my mind while calling "JESUS" or "Father" in my mind.

In my heart, I am calling for GOD the Father that time. I could feel each demon trying to shoot their spiritual self into my mind. Each time, the devils hit a shield GOD placed around me and darted back out like arrows of lighting spearing swiftly from my mind. The demons/fallen angels were around me as I lay there in bed.

One fully black devil in appearance got on the bed next me. I could see this although I could not move or had my eyes open, but apparently was rebuked when I mentally kept repeating "JESUS" "JESUS'… After the devils were rebuked in the name of JESUS by JESUS, I slept better than before. I own a black king Doberman sent by the LORD. This is not the first time demons try to look like my dog in appearance. Months ago, a demon fully black in appearance laid next to me and I did not fear it. I rebuked that devil and all devils in the name of JESUS. Don't be held in bondage to demons. JESUS can set you free.

Most people don't even know they are in demonic bondage. Most people don't even know they are under demonic influence and other seek the influence of demons. GOD gives us free will to choose. Some believers open doors to demons not even knowing they have opened that door. Porn is a door opener for demons to enter. Excessive beer, wine, and liquor are another demonic passage, keeping you bondage. If this is you, find your way to JESUS or back to JESUS. "For GOD so loved the world that He gave His only begotten Son (JESUS) that whosoever believes in Him shall not parish but have everlasting life." Amen. Again, I say this is Grace because JESUS does not want to be separated from His children. Choose to let JESUS enter you and willfully choose eternal life with GOD.

If you are in a position that shame would come your way if your loved ones, your family found out your secret life of …then you are under the influence of an evil spirit (fallen angel kicked out of GOD'S presence. I have met and seen the demons, not by choice and demons have entered me, my family, and JESUS really has cast them out. JESUS said, "Look, I have given you authority over all the power of the enemy (demons), you can walk among snakes and scorpions and crush them. Nothing will injure you." "But don't rejoice because evil spirits obey you; rejoice because your names are registered (written) in heaven." Believers of JESUS, their name is written in the "Lamb's book of life."

Those who do not believe in JESUS are thrown into the lake of fire for eternity. Those who belong to GOD are written in the book of life. Know, JESUS came to set you free. Choose life eternal and not hell eternal. I encourage you to read the Holy Bible. It is not about religion. It is about spirituality with JESUS. If you open the door to demons, they will destroy you.

Though demons can take the form of anything, even the form of an angle of light (holy angel of GOD), or even a deceased or alive family member, we believer's have authority over them by the power of JESUS. Demons do not want you to know this, but it is true. Demons took possession of me when I was 5 and took possession of family members older and younger than me. The demons time is limited and they are trying to take as many people to hell with them. Some people want to go to hell and choose to live with demons on earth, like people who tell you your past or future (mediums). Time on earth is but a moment, a blink of an eye compared to eternal life in the Kingdom of GOD. I tell you truth.
You have two choices, eternal damnation or eternal joyful life with JESUS, are your only two choices. I am witness to, there is a GOD and JESUS lives. GODISJESUSLIVES.

JESUS told me to write these words and testify of the truth. JESUS said, [63]"to open their eyes, in order to turn them from darkness to light, and from the power of satan to GOD, that they may receive forgiveness of sins and an inheritance among those who are sanctified by faith in Me."

[64]"For since the creation of the world His invisible attributes are clearly seen, being understood by the things that are made, even His eternal power and GODHEAD (GOD the Father, GOD the Son, GOD the Holy Spirit), so that they are without excuse, because although they knew GOD, they did not glorify Him as GOD, nor were thankful, but became futile in their thoughts, and their foolish hearts were darkened."

Do not let satan get a hold of you and darken your heart. I met the devil and demons. They are real and hate GOD. They no longer have a choice to be with GOD and are trying to use half-truth and trickery to bring you to their destiny, eternal pain and suffering.

---

[63] Acts 26:18

[64] Romans 1:20

People, mediums as they are called, are speaking to demons. These devils know all about you and your entire family history. They knew are great, great, great Grandparents and so forth. They have tricked me many times. I turn to JESUS before I do anything, and I mean anything. GOD created these fallen angels as he created all things.

I have seen and spoken to demons (in ignorance) and I have seen and spoken with JESUS. The Kingdom of GOD is real. JESUS is real and the only path to the Kingdom of GOD. There are no other ways, no other paths and no other gates, but through JESUS CHRIST.

In the last days before the tribulation, not all of us will die. In the day when JESUS returns to this world, you better have chosen to trust in Him. On that day JESUS will open His mouth and with one word, one breath, JESUS will end all lawlessness and evil of every nature. The fire that will proceed with the sword of JESUS, the breath of His word will destroy the anti-CHRIST and all the people who follow Him, including armies and armies of all nations will be destroyed, parish.

JESUS will cast their spirits into the lake of fire. JESUS will do away with all evil in the sight of GOD.
Righteousness will reign on this new earth. There will be no more pain and suffering at the hands of evil men and evil spirits.

No more evil when the LORD JESUS comes back… JESUS came the first time as the lamb of GOD, but this second time JESUS tells us He is coming back as a Lion to destroy all that is evil on this earth. JESUS tells us all truth. We are JESUS' creatures; we have to answer to sin.

JESUS did not intend for us to be our own democratic organization. JESUS is our Creator. We need JESUS' power, Grace and love. All nations and empires, everyone will fall to JESUS who is our Creator. GODISJESUSLIVES. These are the facts. Remember, "For GOD so loved the world that He gave His only begotten Son, that whoever believes in Him should not perish but have everlasting life."

To all you believers in JESUS, contact me for a divine meal. The LORD GOD JESUS has given me tremendous ability to cook spiritual food He once had my Grandmother's Rebecca and Rachael cook. I call it Manna Earth, Mantilla. I have been gifted with the ability to cook with JESUS. Recipes from JESUS He have given me with no measurements to write.

JESUS "works all spectrums at once" He said to me on April 10, 2018. Do the will of GOD the Father. "And this is the will of Him who sent Me, that everyone who sees the Son and believes in Him may have everlasting life; and I will raise him up at the last day." Don't miss your opportunity to make JESUS your LORD.

Understand the first will be last and the last first. My heart goes out to jack who I mistreated and did not show enough attention to. I showed more attention to my full-blooded Jack Russell terriers and my pure Dobermans than my longhaired golden retriever given to my daughter yet I was left to take care of him and did a very poor job. Now I long to see him first in the Kingdom of GOD. All those neglected believers of JESUS here
on earth will be first in His Kingdom. JESUS opened my eyed to this truth.

Michael Caputo and his family will receive a hundred fold gracious blessings from JESUS. Michael's testimony of

Mueller comes directly from JESUS. It is truth, but don't worry, Robert Mueller [65] and his team of darkness will be thrown into the "Lake of Fire" not before being exposed and punished on earth. Michael, you speak from victory as a son of GOD. Believe [66] "where your treasure is there your heart is too."

Pray for your enemies Michael. Father, In Your Name JESUS I pray all would repent and believe in You JESUS as the Son of GOD as Our Living GOD Who died and Lives. Who defeated death on the cross and by Your blood, all past, present and future sins have been cleaned. Amen. LORD GOD, Amen.

All Pastors of Grace need to remember we and they speak from Victory. JESUS boys and JESUS girls are Victorious. There are no battles as GOD'S children. JESUS defeated death by His body we are healed by His stripes. By the divine blood of JESUS shed at the cross all sins are cleansed at the Cross-, past, present and future sins of this world.

Pastors who teach the Gospel of Grace need remember his congregation is Victorious; there are no battles, just temptations. GODS timing is perfect although there is no such thing as time for GOD. Don't think for a moment JESUS is not allowing these flesh and blood dark light men on earth to continue to harm others. It is part of JESUS realm to expose them all soon.

---

[65] Matthew 6:23-24

[66] Matthew 6:21

Tucker Carlson, son and Laura Ingraham daughter of GOD, a JESUS boy and JESUS girl serving Him well. The Huckabees are a great Christian family. Sarah Huckabee Sanders is a great daughter of God. Father, in Your name JESUS I pray for continued wisdom and knowledge for Your children Tucker, Laura and Sarah. I pray You strengthen their Grace. Amen. Father, in your name JESUS I pray for Tucker, Laura and Sarah Your children's family and those they love. Shower them with joy and happiness, and continued shield of protection from wolves dressed in sheep clothing. May they be surround by those who love You and witness to those who do not know You. Amen.

Sarah, don't worry about Jim Acosta, the lost CNN soul who is heading to the pit where there will be "gnashing of teeth" and total darkness for eternity. Our job is to pray for him. Father in Your name JESUS I pray that You help Your son Jim overcome the darkness that dwells in him. I pray he gets saved before Your coming by repenting. May salvation be his. Amen.

I look at people like him and only focus at how lost they are and how much they are of this world. Do you want truth Jim? If you were to die right now, would you go to be with JESUS? All these people are JESUS boys and girls, brother and sisters in the Kingdom of GOD. Know JESUS' Will will be done. Amen.

Robert Mueller and his tribe of luciferians do not understand the country does not care about sins forgiven him by JESUS. JESUS cares for all and the devil uses people like Mueller to hurt others then the devil discards Mueller and laughs in his face. JESUS cleaned all past, present, and future sins of President Trump. Condemnation is Robert Mueller's middle name.

The military says GOD, then Country... what they need to say is JESUS then country, because GOD the Father wants all to believe Him when He says, "Through His (JESUS) name, whoever believes in Him will receive remission of sins." Change your ways. Believe in JESUS and you will receive forgiveness of sins. Sins you were already born with. We were all born with the curse of sin. Believe JESUS died for our sins. All sins were transferred to Him, and His righteousness transferred to us. Rest in knowing that JESUS saved you. Give up your self-righteousness and know there is no other way to eternal life of joy.

The New Covenant with GOD cost the death of JESUS, His Son. We are blessed with the Blessings of CHRIST JESUS. JESUS was obedient to GOD the Father. In JESUS' obedience and blessing we have eternal life in the Kingdom of GOD. We are viewed Holy (dedicated to GOD) by GOD and we are viewed blameless by GOD after the death of JESUS and once you are born again, saved. The warfare with the devil is ongoing. The evil spirits seek to have you think differently. The evil spirits, the devil seeks to have you think, GOD does not love you.

The devil wants you to think you are not saved and you are not born again. The devil wants you to think you can save yourself and not the Spirit of GOD. The devil will always try to take the focus off JESUS and put the focus on you. That is why lucifer (the devil) and the fallen angels were thrown out of the Kingdom of GOD, for thinking, they could tell the Creator (GOD) that they could be gods.
Make no mistake, I met and have spoken to the devil and demons and they use trickery to trick us. The devil is able to throw thoughts into our minds. JESUS is our GOD and He is our Creator. JESUS is the Word and "the Word was with GOD, and the Word was GOD." The life of Faith is stretched to every living person. The Gospel of the Kingdom of GOD gives us faith.

JESUS is the source of love, light and eternal life for us all. JESUS said, "I am the bread of life. He who comes to Me shall never hunger, and he who believes in Me shall never thirst." It is all about JESUS and our faith in Him who GOD the Father sent to save us from death to hell eternal. JESUS even tells one of His disciples Thomas, who said unless he literally saw and felt JESUS' resurrected self, he would not believe.

JESUS did appear to Thomas and asked Thomas to, "Reach your finger here, and look at My hands; and reach your hand here, and put it into My side (the parts of JESUS' body He had been stabbed), do not be unbelieving but believing." Thomas then believed and praised JESUS as his LORD and GOD. JESUS said, "Thomas, because you have seen Me, you have believed. Blessed are those who have not seen and yet believed." I have seen JESUS and JESUS spoke to me. JESUS called me, "daughter." I belong to JESUS and the devil cannot "snatch' what belongs to GOD Almighty.

I am reminded of Psalm 56, "Be merciful to me, my GOD, for my enemies are in hot pursuit; all day long they press their attack. My adversaries pursue me all day long; in their pride many are attacking me. When I am afraid, I put my trust in you. In GOD, whose word I praise—in GOD I trust and am not afraid. What can mere mortals do to me? All day long, they twist my words; all their schemes are for my ruin. They conspire, they lurk, and they watch my steps, hoping to take my life. Because of their wickedness do not let them escape; in your anger, GOD, bring the nations down. Record my misery; list my tears on your scroll— are they not in your record? Then my enemies will turn back when I call for help. By this I will know that <u>GOD is for me</u>. In GOD, whose word I praise, in the LORD, whose word I praise—in GOD I trust and am not afraid. What can man do to me? I am under vows to you, my GOD; I will present my thank offerings to you. For you have delivered me from death and my feet from stumbling, that I may walk before GOD in the light of life." Amen (so be it.).

[67]"Greater is He that is in me, then he that is in the world." We are of GOD. I say this to you and all as a daughter of GOD. Believers' know what I am saying to those GOD loves, but are not saved. Even Jews whose belief in Judaism which all is meaningless unless you are born again in and through CHRIST JESUS.

King Solomom, the wisest man ever created by GOD, also son of King David a man after GOD'S own heart said, [68]" And moreover, because the Preacher (him) was wise, he still taught the people knowledge; yes he pondered and sought out and set in order many proverbs. The preacher sought to find acceptable words; and what were written was upright-words of truth. The words of the wise are like goads, and the words of scholars are like well-driven nails, given by one Shepard. And further, my son, be admonished by these. Of making many books there is no end, and much study is wearisome to the flesh. Let us hear the conclusion of the whole matter: Fear GOD and keep His Commandments, For this is man's all. For GOD will bring every work into judgment, including every secret thing, Whether good or evil."

All is *meaningless* if JESUS is not your LORD and Savior. King Salomon, King David and JESUS are from the tribe of Judah, as I too have Tribe of Judah and Tribe of Benjamin blood, forced into Roman Catholicism-all meaningless.

---

[67] 1John 4:4

[68] Ecclesiastes 12:9

I became a Christian in CHRIST JESUS, which is meaningful. It gave me eternal life with GOD in His Kingdom. Let the Holy angels rejoice by your choosing of life with JESUS. Choose JESUS. Know that the devil is liar 24/7, and does it through people, and mixes truth to trick you. People who lie all the time have a lying spirit. Sometimes the devil will say something over the phone/cell to stumble you into being of this world.

The devil wants to confuse you at all times. The stronger the faith the more demonic attacks. That is why I have learned to discern which is which, of the devil. One time, I was talking to Verizon and at the end of establishing an account the person said, thank Ms. Baumann. " a former name not told to Verizon. It was the devil trying to get me side tracked. Like I said, the devil has called me on the phone, said, "Hi Yvonne", and has whispered my name in my ear.

I thank GOD through JESUS CHRIST that He removed the spirit of fear from my body, from me totally in 2000 while I was taking a shower. I literally felt it go off my body and down the drain. That was how JESUS chose to do it and it was GOD who told me what had happened. I did not know what He meant or what the spirit of fear was, until I was tormented by evil spirits for years onward and did not react fearfully. I did not know about rebuking, commanding the evil fallen angels to depart from me in the powerful name of JESUS until 2009.

JESUS told me prior to my February 2013 fusion surgery in my neck that I would "heal swiftly" and I would have "much to say." I do have much to say and I am bold to speak of my LORD JESUS. I love you LORD JESUS. JESUS has me speaking then and now. There was even a time while I slept that evil spirits were tormenting me, boxing me in to where I could not move, my spirit yelled, "Father" and they fled. The demons were rebuked by, GOD the Father. I am a daughter of the Living GOD. I am spiritual royalty. After this life I have a mansion waiting for me in the Kingdom of GOD.

6

JESUS APPEARED
DARKNESS FLEES WHEN LIGHT APPROACHES
IVANKA TRUMP AND GRACE

I live in Hungry Horse, Montana. Hungry horse is the Nazareth of Montana. The territory is beautiful; we are the lowly of the lowliest. Every other day is a shooting sometimes killings. Every one knows everyone. I love Hungry Horse. I have traveled the world, and this is the most beautiful and my home. We are protective of one another. The only people who choose to hate me are Jehovah Witnesses and Mormons. Smith pharmacy (Mormons) in Columbia Falls just five minutes away is a near perfect example of hatred towards others seeded by lucifer. Seeds of doubt are laid by demons here. Meth and illegal drugs is rampage between Montana and Washington State. Even so, many JESUS lovers live here. Ex-Mormons for JESUS in Orange California is doing work for JESUS. Mormons do not acknowledge the "cross" JESUS died on. It is a symbol of eternal Life.

GOD is GOD the Father, GOD the Son and GOD the Holy Spirit. One GOD; three divine Persons in GOD.. The Holy Spirit is GOD. JESUS the Son is GOD. Father is GOD. After the crucifixion and resurrection of JESUS, He sent the Holy Spirit. The Holy Spirit has a will and that is the will of GOD. He is fully GOD. He is eternal. GOD the Father, GOD our LORD JESUS, and GOD the Holy Spirit.

GOD Is, omnipresent (present everywhere at the same tine), and omniscient (knows everything). The Holy Spirit is all knowing, all wise and all seeing. The Holy Spirit lives in me and in all believers. The Holy Spirit bears witness of JESUS.

Just like we have a soul, body and spirit-three in one, it is not hard to accept, feel and believe that GOD is, three persons, but One GOD. You can know the will of GOD by asking the Holy Spirit who intercedes for us believers, us children of GOD. The fruit (attributes) of the Holy Spirit are "love, joy, peace, forbearance, Skindness, goodness, faithfulness, gentleness, and self-control." People are baptized in the name of GOD the Father, GOD the Son and GOD the Holy Spirit. The Holy Spirit inspires our prayers to communicate with GOD. The Holy Spirit leads the children of GOD.

The Holy Spirit empowers the children of GOD. The Holy Spirit convicts us when we are doing wrong, sinning in eyes of GOD. The Holy Spirit gave me the gift of being a faith healer and gives spiritual gifts to the children of GOD. The Holy Spirit helps us overcome the desires of the flesh. The Holy Spirit teaches us to stand upright. The Holy Spirit gives us strength.

[69] "Do not grieve the Holy Spirit of GOD, by whom you were sealed for the day of redemption." Lying grieves the Holy Spirit of GOD, "let each one of you speak truth with his neighbor," ... "let all bitterness, wrath, anger, clamor, and evil speaking be put away from you, with all malice." "And be kind to one another, tenderhearted, forgiving one another, even as GOD in CHRIST forgave you."

When you are saved you realize that JESUS has already forgiven you for your sins and expects you to try not to sin. Remember we are all born sinners since Adam's downfall when he disobeyed GOD. Believers are sealed by, the Holy Spirit of GOD until the day of redemption. When we sin, it grieves the Holy Spirit. We don't lose our salvation when we sin, we will see GOD the Father, GOD the Son and GOD the Holy Spirit when we are redeemed.

---

[69] Ephesians 4:30

JESUS took our sins away past, present and future. JESUS did everything right in the eyes of GOD. We do wrong and fall short, yet GOD sees us as He sees JESUS, righteous. The Holy Spirit of GOD wants fellowship with you at all times. The Holy Spirit cannot fellowship with us when we are walking on the path of sinful acts, darkness. Choose fellowship with the Holy Spirit. Don't defile your soul. Set yourself apart from your continued sin. We are loved by, the Holy Spirit of GOD. Don't be prideful. Humility is a good thing. We know what GOD'S will is at present time through the Holy Spirit.

Get to know the Holy Spirit of GOD so you can grow in Faith. He will direct you to honor GOD. GOD'S children can hear GOD. GOD speaks to us all, listen and hear Him. A friend once asked GOD, "are you real?" GOD replied to her, "are you real?" Wow! GOD makes His point with few words. "Through His (JESUS) name, whoever believes in Him will receive remission of sins." Whoever believes in Him is a perquisite to repentance. Believe in JESUS. JESUS is the good news.

The gift of having the Holy Spirit in you are for all people of this world. Psalm 19 says, *"The heavens declare the glory of GOD; the skies proclaim the work of his hands. Day after day they pour forth speech; night after night they reveal knowledge. They have no speech, they use no words; no sound is heard from them. Yet their voice goes out into all the earth, their words to the ends of the world. In the heavens GOD has pitched a tent for the sun. It is like a bridegroom coming out of his chamber, like a champion rejoicing to run his course. It rises at one end of the heavens and makes its circuit to the other; nothing is deprived of its warmth. The law of the LORD is perfect, refreshing the soul. The statutes of the LORD are trustworthy, making wise the simple. The precepts of the LORD are right, giving joy to the heart. The commands of the LORD are radiant, giving light to the eyes. The fear of the LORD is pure, enduring forever.*

The decrees of the LORD are firm, and all of them are righteous. They are more precious than gold, than much pure gold; they are sweeter than honey, than honey from the honeycomb. By them your servant is warned; in keeping them there is great reward. But who can discern their own errors? Forgive my hidden faults. Keep your servant also from willful sins; may they not rule over me. Then I will be blameless, innocent of great transgression. May these words of my mouth and this meditation of my heart be pleasing in your sight, LORD, my Rock and my Redeemer." JESUS belongs to all. We all belong to JESUS. He created each one of us.

Demons choose to appear ugly and shake homes and furniture. They choose to blow humans minds. The gorier they appear the more scared and fearful humans are. Demons and fallen angels including lucifer (satan), is also a creation of GOD, as we are. GOD gave them immortal life, which ends in an eternal lake of fire where they will spend eternity. They can appear as ghosts, as people we know whether dead or alive.

When you have JESUS in your life, the fallen angels cannot harm you. When you have deep faith in JESUS, the fallen angels try using false evidence appearing real. No fear by them can overcome the power of JESUS. Command all evil to be gone in the name of JESUS. There is power in His name. Noted: soon after writing the above, fallen angels started throwing things around in my bedroom.

My dog and I were sitting in the living room and all of a sudden, things thrown around trying to scare me. I walked into the bedroom and immediately JESUS rebuked them, further casting them into the [70]abyss chain bound and gagged until judgment day. GOD in me, me in JESUS, JESUS in GOD, GOD in JESUS, we are one.

---

[70] Revelation 9:2

Remember, [71] "For GOD did not send His Son (JESUS) into the world to condemn the world, but that the world through Him might be saved. He who believes in Him is not condemned, but he who does not believe is condemned already, because he has not believed in the name of the only begotten Son of GOD." GOD the Son, JESUS said this not man. I said earlier, JESUS is more than a prophet. Again, JESUS the Son of GOD said, [72]"And this is the condemnation, that the light has come into the world, and men loved darkness rather that light, because their deeds were evil." Have no fear once you are in CHRIST JESUS.

Do not let the devil rob you of the truth by allowing the devil to throw evil and fearful thoughts into your mind. The devil cannot read your thoughts and is very cunning, throws thoughts into your mind waiting for a preplanned action. Us believer's will judge the fallen angels, those devils, those fallen angels who try to torment us.

The death of JESUS, all people can be saved. Confess with words, JESUS I believe you are the Son of GOD. I believe You are GOD in the flesh sent by GOD the Father. I believe You gave your life freely and laid it down at the cross where You where crucified for our sins. You JESUS, took our place of judgment and died for the remission of my sins. You took my judgment upon yourself. I believe JESUS is my LORD and Savior and my GOD. I believe JESUS rose again in fulfillment of the Holy Scriptures. I believe JESUS is resurrected and is seated at the right hand of our Heavenly Father GOD. I believe JESUS will come again. All sins, including the most evil, despicable were judged at the cross and paid for by JESUS.

---

[71] John 3:17

[72] John 3:19

Stay away from all institutes that live on political correctness. For a person outside of CHRIST JESUS, non-believers, when you die your going to stand before GOD, He will judge you and the gospel says you will be thrown into hell forever and ever. People will be yelling for another chance to choose JESUS, it will be too late at that point. Right now choose life eternal. GOD loves us. GOD forgives sin when you are born again by accepting JESUS by faith.

Again, faith in JESUS is accepting JESUS as the Son of GOD. Say, JESUS, I believe you are the Son of GOD. I believe You are GOD in the flesh sent by GOD the Father. I believe You gave your life freely and laid it down at the cross where You where crucified for our sins. JESUS took our place of judgment, died for the remission of my sins, and took my judgment upon you. I believe JESUS is my LORD and Savior and my GOD. I believe JESUS rose again in fulfillment of the Holy Scriptures. I believe JESUS is resurrected and is seated at the right hand of our Heavenly Father GOD. I believe JESUS will come again. JESUS I believe, "For GOD so loved the world that He gave His only begotten Son (JESUS) that whosoever believes in Him shall not parish but have everlasting life." Amen. Have a personal faith in CHRIST JESUS.

Know without a doubt that when JESUS the creator GOD Himself, took on human flesh, He died that death by crucifixion, pouring-out all of His wrath for sin, from Adam until the last person in time. Their sin was laid on CHRIST JESUS on the cross and GOD judged it, and poured out His wrath on JESUS.

Again, JESUS is our redeemer. Remember JESUS is Grace. Once, and for all, we believers have been crucified with CHRIST JESUS.

Paul (previous named Saul) wrote most of the New Testament for JESUS, GOD. When JESUS was preaching on earth, He often time preached "under the law" to the Jews. After His death on the cross, and rose from the dead, He told His disciples to [73] "Go into all the world, and preach the gospel to every creature." I even told my wonderful pet dogs about JESUS.

Dogs can sense evil and see fallen angels too. Mine did and was hit on the head for barking at that demon. My Mom saw it happen, but could not see the demon at the time it happened. It came back to my mother in the form of a deceased person and smiled at my Mom then disappeared. They, the demons do that sort of stuff all of the time putting fear in people or tricking them into believing that they are that person in the form of a spirit. Don't be tricked. Rebuke them in the name of JESUS and watch them disappear. Cast them into the pit chain bound and gagged unto judgment day by our LORD JESUS.

Raised as a gentile-a non-Jew. I did not know I was a Jew until several years ago. I am certain my parents who died in 2008 and 2011 did not know either. I am certain their parents did not know either. They were forced into Roman Catholicism! Nonetheless, we are all GOD'S chosen people. We are His people and He is our GOD. GOD is miraculous. GOD foresees our path and makes life a blessing.

This is my happening of the transforming from darkness into light. It has taken many failures and disappointments in life to get my attention. It has taken failed marriages, ill relations and devastations to wonder about GOD. It has taken medical health problems to get me to wonder if I should read something as important as the Holy Bible.

---

[73] Mark 16:15

It took the death of my mother, then my father, then the abandonment of my immediate family for me to ask another question to GOD. "Where are my Parents?"

2001 I saw JESUS. He showed me to carry my cross onto the path He leads. Tears were cried by local women in dark mourning clothes as they watched JESUS walk by with the Cross dragging a foot behind Him of the cobblestone road. The cross section laid on JESUS left shoulder as he carried the Cross as He walked down a narrow cobblestone path curved to his left. Cross on His shoulder dragging a foot or two behind Him on the cobblestone.

JESUS was knocking on my [74] door and still, I did not open it or call His name at heart. JESUS appeared to me, therefore; I give testimony as a witness that GODISJESUSLIVES.

I literally saw JESUS and not in a vision or a dream, but in person. JESUS appeared to me to give testimony He lives. Give JESUS the key to every door in your life and the key to your heart. Let there be no exceptions to the areas of your life JESUS may enter. Read the "Sermon on the Mount" JESUS gave us. JESUS covers all aspects of our lives in that sermon. JESUS makes it clear all aspects of your life are where He is. Give JESUS the master key to be.

Do not put JESUS in a box. I share truth with you because I am being obedient to JESUS. He chose this sinner to share the truth with you. JESUS wants all to be saved and to be born again in the Spirit of GOD. Choose life eternal with Grace. Otherwise, you will end up with lucifer and his demons in the pit eternally, where there is utter darkness and suffering.

The pit is not just for evil people, but also for nice caring non-believers in JESUS CHRIST. We have this knowledge beforehand; now have the faith to believe in JESUS. GOD gives us all free will to choose.

---

[74] Matthew 7:9

Going to church religiously without faith in JESUS, is not going to save you from judgment. GOD knows your heart, if you are not born again. You have to walk the truth and not just talk the motion. JESUS loves you. Love Him back. Ask JESUS questions. He will answer you. You do not need a priest or church leader to speak directly to JESUS; you do need JESUS to speak to GOD.

Ivanka Trump, what a gracious blessing to us all. She will not be separated from JESUS, or from her children unlike Samantha Bee, a jealous coward. Ashley Judd, has been coward and Madonna, a washed up coward. All three are traitors to women of JESUS, to all JESUS girls. Y'all are children of your father the devil. You are all luciferians. The words that precede y'alls mouth is meaningless to all, but your doom in the realm our JESUS lives. It is "what comes out of the mouth" that hurts you and your LORD GOD JESUS. Ivanka will be in the Kingdom of GOD. Father I pray in Your name JESUS that you show Your lost daughters the path to salvation, to repentance. Amen.

Andrew Weissman, you are not wise at all. Repent and put JESUS before your idolizations of false power, false recognition and temporary wealth. Remember all you luciferians, giving to charities and dumb speeches to not lead to salvation.

This world is coming to an end and in my generation. The rapture will happen within 14 years according to what JESUS has told me (May, 2032 is an important month and year), and Armageddon soon after.

"Daughter, No One Called My Name"

This is a message from JESUS to all you lost luciferians. I cried wanting to be there in the synagogue when JESUS read from the "The Book of Isaiah,"[75]"Today this scripture is fulfilled in your hearing." Wow, to have been there to hear JESUS...I cried wanting badly to have heard Him in person proclaim He is GOD. That is when JESUS told me I would partake in the rapture. How loved I am by JESUS to spare me from dieing here on earth, rather I shall be one blessed to be caught up in the clouds during the rapture in the blink of an eye.

On March 18, 2018, I was sleeping and while asleep and in the spirit (1st vision) I sat up on my bed, glanced over to my right and saw the bottom half of my toothbrush holder. A cactus plant one inch in diameter grew out of it about six inches, then another horn of the cactus plant grew out of that one. It forms a slanted Y with prickly cactus thorns. I watched it fall slowly over the edge of my bed. I turned to my left and grabbed my light and flashed it to the floor where I witnessed the [76]two-horn cactus had fallen, but did not see it. It was gone.

Soon after (2nd vision) I found myself in a room, a house belonging to the Trump family filled with important people and his family. I witnessed President Trump (World leader) drive up with Roger De Coster (crowned a Knight from Belgium by the King of Belgium) in a red sports car. Belgium represents the United Nations. President Trump represents the USA.

Then still while in the spirit I am in a room by myself with ten small rocks. I slowly grab one knowing there is a jewel in the center. I try with both hands to crumble the rock to get the jewel in the center but it wont crumble. I slowly grab another rock and it wont crumble.

---

[75] Luke 4:17-21

[76] Revelation 13:11

I grab a third rock and it crumbles easily leaving a brilliant "Lazul" brilliant sapphire in the palm of my hand. This sapphire represents GOD'S Throne in the Kingdom of Heaven. I do not know the meaning of it taking 3 rocks for GOD'S Throne to be revealed to me via the sapphire from the 3rd stone…

The next morning JESUS interpreted the visions for me. He said the 1st vision represented the anti CHRIST will be coming soon and will be defeated, never to be found again. The 2nd vision represented JESUS' Kingdom will be here shortly to rule His children. No other nations will be. This is a wake up call for all leaders, for all nations, for all evil people to repent and believe in JESUS as GOD.

Choose JESUS or choose hell. Works will not get you into His Kingdom. I and many other believers know the time is at hand. The rapture is coming within 14 years. This world is ending soon after and in my generation; however, I and other children of GOD will be rapture and resurrected to be with JESUS.

Joseph Prince and all Grace gospel teachers have been told this happening by JESUS. Turn to GOD by repenting and believing in His Son JESUS CHRIST.

This morning I was laughing with GOD on misunderstanding how I thought it was my compassionate nature He was referring to when I several years ago I asked GOD "why" "why me?" GOD said one word to me, "compassion." Nothing I could have done alone would have given me salvation. Because of GOD'S compassion for me, I get to spend eternity with Him. Wow! I am not worthy to be the daughter of GOD, but that is not true to GOD. He did not see me as unworthy. GOD sees no man alive as unworthy.

GOD'S compassion extends to us all equally. This I know cause He told me so. I was dead and now I am alive in JESUS. I have been so disrespectful and selfish, now I am born again and saved and will spend eternity with JESUS because of His love and Grace and mercy. Before I was born again, saved GOD the Father, JESUS had His arms wide open, waiting for me to be. Do not let the door close on you, become a new creature by confessing with your mouth that JESUS is Lord and gave His life for the remission of sins.

Believe in your heart that JESUS is LORD. GOD wants us now as sinners. Do not have earthly thoughts of waiting to get your act together, allow GOD, allow JESUS who is GOD to help you every step of the way to living as you ought to. Overcome the evil spirits and declare victory. We are not perfect, but even with our flaws we can declare that we are children of GOD Almighty. The truth is, GOD loves me, and you just the way we are.

Go home to GOD He is waiting. There are no other GODS. One true GOD waiting with His arms wide open. There is nothing more important than spending eternal life with GOD. Nothing.

Experience an awaking and go home to GOD spiritually. GOD knows who you are, where you come from and what you have done; yet He still waits for you with love. JESUS is the way. Join me and other believers in the Kingdom of GOD.

Do not miss GODS Grace. Put all your confidence in GODS Grace. Unbelievers are dead to truth. Believe and live. Through JESUS we are given the love and Grace undeserving to us. Read GODS Holy Bible. Read for yourself where you will go after death on earth. The Holy Bible is about our past, present and future.

GOD relentlessly loves all of us. GOD wants all to be saved. Understand that GOD loves us all the same equally. Trust in JESUS. Choose life, not hell. Choose eternal life and not eternal hell. Trust in your Creator, JESUS. Do not be separated from your Creator. You will know when you are saved. You will feel the Grace of GOD inside you and no one can take it away from you.

    Know this Elon Musk, GOD did not give you or anyone else dominion of the universe and certainly not Mars. [77] Dominion of Earth and only Earth is given his children, although we are[78] citizens of Heaven. You are heading for disaster and so is Stormy Daniels who has little time to repent and believe in JESUS.

    Three months before Election Day for Flathead County Sheriff, JESUS woke me up as He always does and told me to write Brian Heino. JESUS had me send a letter saying he would become the next sheriff and to pray before he judged GOD'S children. Yesterday's paper (headline: Brian Heino elected Sheriff) quoted our newly elected sheriff, but not once did Brian thank GOD. He did not give thanks to JESUS. GOD had me send him another letter yesterday (June 6, 2018) saying JESUS put him in that position.

    Keith Stahlberg is indeed a JESUS boy and although he was not elected Sheriff, he won the powerball of knowing he will be in the Kingdom of Heaven. Only GOD knows why He has me doing what He has me doing and saying about His children. Some will heed His warning and some will go directly to hell for not listening to the truth of JESUS.

---

[77] Genesis 1:26

[78] Philippians 3:20

7

ONLY TWO CHOICES, ETERNAL LIFE WITH JESUS OR ETERNAL HELL WHERE EVERYONE IS A BELIEVER IN JESUS.

Be comforted in knowing that GOD protects His children and His protection shall never pass away. There are evil angels and good angels all around us at all times. What you read and what you watch can be harmful, so ask JESUS about all before acting on your own. The Kingdom of GOD and eternal hell is the only two choices you have. There is a fine line between the two choices. Choose the Kingdom of GOD. Do not be fooled by the evil angels pretending to be what they are not. One even told me he knew me in heaven before I was born and that we studied together at a university in heaven. Those are the lies of an evil demon or satan himself. What matters is right now. Are you going to choose JESUS or are you going to choose one of the evil angels who pretend it has powers over JESUS.
You will meet JESUS face to face and you will know what I tell you are truth. Read the word of the Living GOD. GOD Almighty created us from dirt and breathed soul into us all.

There is GOD and He is powerful. There is no end to His world or His existence. GOD is three in one. GOD is the Father, GOD is JESUS the Son and GOD is the Holy Spirit. That is plain and simple to understand. We answer to no prophet. We answer to GOD JESUS the Messiah. JESUS is the Messiah.

JESUS is a leader and the Savior of all people not just Jews. JESUS saved us Christians from eternal hell. JESUS delivered us all from our sins. JESUS did not save only Jews. Abraham was not a Jew. JESUS of Nazareth is our King and the Messiah who is the anointed by GOD His Father to save us from death and eternal suffering.

Pray for understanding of what is being said in this message from GODISJESUSLIVES. JESUS CHRIST is translated and same as JESUS the Messiah. All things visible and invisible were created by, GOD for and through JESUS. Things not seen are greater than things seen. We live in a temporary world that we can see. The invisible world is far greater than our visible world. Do not be fooled by evil angles.

Evil angels know they made the wrong choice for death and destruction leading all of them to eternal hell, eternal suffering. Evil angels try to take as many of GODS children as they can. Evil angels hate GODS children. I am not a preacher or teacher, or evangelist. I am a child of GOD giving testimony of what I have seen and know to be true. I have seen evil angels and I have seen JESUS. The Kingdom of GOD is real. Hell is real. The gospel of GOD is truth. I have seen holy angels. These holy angels had no wings. Understand we were all created by, GOD for our Lord JESUS, and in and through JESUS. Angels are everywhere. GOD is everywhere. When you are born again, a child of GOD, GOD protects you with His power. We are under the protection of JESUS. Make JESUS a part of your process of living. [79]GOD promised protection. GOD shall "give His holy angels charge over us to protect us from our enemies."

The gift of righteousness is from GOD. GOD made His Son CHRIST JESUS who was without sin to be sin, so that born again Christians, believers would, "become the righteousness of GOD." Holy angels are mighty in power when carrying out the judgment of GOD. Do not be left behind when the tribulation starts. The tribulation is upon us all. If you are born again, you will not have to endure the tribulation.

---

[79] Psalm 91

The tribulation is suffering, pain, distress, misery, great sadness, grief, and heartache all rolled into one emotion. It will be a trying experience to come. The great tribulation is real. Non-believers will be tested before the arrival of JESUS. Some people will come out of this testing and trial, but a vast majority will not. The Holy bible tells us one-third of the human race will be destroyed in a day. Only GOD knows the day and hour this will occur. GOD tells us soon. There are approximately 7-8 billion people on earth today. Approximately 3 billion people will be wiped out completely. That is many souls gone in one day. GOD is not intimidated by, things He created. GOD is JESUS and JESUS is divine, not a creation of GOD.

The evil angels were holy before they became evil. GOD is going to destroy all evil and answers to no creation. Global tribulation is almost here. GOD is going to release His angels to crush the ungodly and once again, the world will know He is GOD. JESUS is GOD. There is no other. No other.

GOD of heaven is with us born again, with us believers of JESUS. We are not alone. GOD does not slumber nor sleep. GOD'S children worship Him and that is the purpose of His angels too. There are holy angels before the throne of GOD always worshipping Him. There is no time or night and day before the throne of GOD, but Glorious light 24/7.

JESUS tells us to watch for, so not be fooled by the anti-CHRIST. JESUS said, "and you will hear of wars and threats of wars, but Do not panic. Yes, these things must take place, but the end will not follow immediately. Nation will go to war against kingdom. There will be famines and earthquakes in many parts of the world."

This is the beginning of the awaited second coming of JESUS CHRIST. Be one of the people saved and born again. I give testimony of JESUS this side of heaven. JESUS is alive and is our GOD. JESUS is our Lord and KING. The only way to save yourself is to put your faith in JESUS. The devil is going to try to trip you up GOD and that He is our Lord and SAVIOR, then you are going straight to hell which is called the [80]"second death." It will be eternally too late to accept JESUS when you see Him after your first death, if your dead when He comes back, the "second coming" of CHRIST JESUS. You will spend eternity in hell with other non-believers in JESUS and the already existing evil angels.

GOD has already told us that all people who do not believe in JESUS will spend eternity in hell. It is simple to understand, but hard for people to get away from thinking about eternity existence. [81]You will exist eternally. Are you choosing for hell or for the Kingdom of GOD? GOD gives us freedom to[82]choose. I choose life eternal with GOD. I choose the truth. The truth is the truth. JESUS is Lord and Savior. Only GOD who is JESUS could and did save us from eternal hell, and gave us another choice. JESUS has given us all an option to choose eternal life with GOD.

We do not have the understanding or the knowledge GOD has and never will. We know that GOD created us, and all things. We know we were created by, GOD and for GOD. GOD is a divine Spirit. We know CHRIST came to earth in the form of a person with flesh and gave His divine blood, JESUS born fully Man.

---

[80] Revelation 20:14

[81] Daniel 12:2,3; Matthew 25:46; John 5:28; Revelation 20:14,15

[82] Romans 1:18,21 & 25

We know that GOD knows the end to the beginning and His world has no end. We know that GOD gave us all a way out of hell eternal, and that way out leads to eternal life with Him. Two choices are all. Do not let one of the evil angles fool you by having you think wrong. Or believing GOD could lie to us. GOD cannot lie. You being created by GOD cannot save yourself from eternal hell, apart from GOD. GOD compassionately gave us a path to live with Him eternally. It is GODS desire that all be saved.

JESUS knows the end to the beginning of creation. He told us many people do not find the path to Him. Gee whiz, GOD gives us the heads up. If you want to avoid eternal suffering after you die then have faith in JESUS and what GOD has told us to do in order to avoid eternal hell where there will be[83] gnashing of teeth from all the pain and suffering.

If you were to die right now, where would you go, Heaven or hell? I am going to heaven and I will live in the Kingdom of GOD. Right now, accept the truth, have the faith. Accept the truth and choose faith in JESUS. JESUS gave His life for the remission (cancellation of debt) of sins (our sins past, present and future – penalty of hell). Believe in your heart GOD raised JESUS from the dead. This is true. Truth will lead you to faith in JESUS. You will be saved.

JESUS freely gives us salvation. This is the spirit of faith. When you choose to believe in JESUS, then salvation is yours and cannot be taken away from you. JESUS already paid the ransom, the price. If you do not choose the truth of JESUS, you will end up in hell and no one is able to remove you from your eternal home, hell.

---

[83] Matthew 8:12; 13:50; Mark 9:48

Being saved, born again does not mean you are perfect and cannot sin. It does give us the divine promise that GOD sees us as He sees JESUS, perfect. You do not have to have the full understanding and knowledge of the Holy Bible to be saved.

Some people saved surpass pastors and priest in knowledge. Some people preach the Holy Bible without understanding. Save yourself and start reading the only book on earth that matters. Then help others save themselves.

For in it the righteousness of GOD is revealed from faith to faith, as it is written, "but the righteous man shall live by Faith." Live by faith and let JESUS do for you all He can. There is only one way to heaven. JESUS is the only way to heaven. Faith in JESUS CHRIST is the only way to heaven. Do not suffer the eternal results of separation from GOD. The gospel is the power of GOD giving us all knowledge for salvation. GOD loves us all.

All I need is Lord GOD JESUS. He is alive. He is our Lord. Go to prayer. Repent and turn away from your voluntary sins. If you turn away from your sinful nature, JESUS is there to enter your heart and save you. With all your heart and mind, believe in JESUS. You will see and feel a change in your life. Accept JESUS as your Lord and SAVIOR. In GOD we trust. "If we confess our sins, He is faithful and just, to forgive us our sins and to cleanse us from all unrighteousness."

Almighty GOD sent His Son JESUS CHRIST from heaven to this earth to take our sins and rescue us. JESUS took our sins while He died on the cross and shed His blood to cover us with His righteousness. JESUS was buried and raised in three days to life by GOD His Father. GOD Is our Father. JESUS Lives. JESUS will go into every heart of those willing to welcome Him. Invite and trust JESUS and welcome Him into your heart.

The message of the Holy Bible is to turn from your sins. Welcome and trust JESUS into your heart. GOD wants all to be saved and united with Him. GOD is giving this message to the end of the earth. GODS book has stood the test since the beginning of time. Give your life to JESUS and ask Him to be your Lord, your SAVIOR. What would happen to you if today were your last day on earth? Where would you go? Are you willing to take a chance of time being on your side? Accidents do happen and evil is always trying to devour people. Where would you spend eternity? If you die now, eternity is what is next for you. Would you spend eternity with GOD or with the devil?

GOD wants all his children in His Kingdom where there is peace and joy. Alternatively, suffer with satan in fire of anguish, eternal pain and suffering. There is a Kingdom to gain and a hell to shun. Two thousand years ago on the cross, JESUS shed the divine blood and paid the price for you to avoid the devil's hell. Today you can change your eternal path by accepting JESUS into your heart and living by faith. Trust in JESUS. JESUS stands with arms wide open because of His love for you. JESUS says come to me.

JESUS will give you rest. JESUS calls you today. I am talking about a relationship with JESUS and not a religion. Religion is vanity by man. Humble yourself and go to JESUS. Believe the truth, JESUS loves you so very much. The word of GOD declares, "For GOD so loved the world that He gave His only begotten Son, that whoever believes in Him should not perish but have everlasting life." Surrender your life to JESUS. Say, JESUS, come and be my Lord and SAVIOR. Tell Him you are tired of a life of sin. Tell Him you surrender your life to Him (JESUS) today. Tell Him you repent of your sins and ask Him to be Lord of your life. JESUS will come and save you. You will be born again and I will see you in His Kingdom.

Even if you have given your life to JESUS and have backslide, recommit your life to Him. The Lord JESUS says you can come back to Him and He will use you to save others. JESUS calls you and only JESUS can see your heart. Do not let pride, lust, jealousy, or anger take control of you. The devil uses your weaknesses against you. The devil wants you to think JESUS will not accept you. Lies by the devil will stumble you. Allow JESUS to talk to you and show you He will take you no matter what you have done.

All forgivable by JESUS, no matter what has happened and transpired in your life. Do not let a storm of a sudden divorce; lost of a loved one or job, sudden illness betrayal of a close family member or friend, trickery by satan, whatever knocks the wind out of you, let JESUS think for you and not you. Do not be stuck alone. JESUS will help you instantly. You can give your life to JESUS afresh. Let today be a new beginning for you.

GOD wants you to be hot for Him. This is the time to be hot for GOD, not cold or lukewarm, but hot for JESUS. Now is the time to surrender to JESUS. JESUS calls you today. Be healed by the power of GOD. Fall in love with JESUS or comeback to JESUS. Do not let the devil lie to you and tell you your not saved. GOD will give you salvation or restore the joy of your salvation. Step aside darkness, there is power in light, and JESUS is light.

JESUS is healing. I said earlier, JESUS kept nudging me to heal that person or this person with His name said aloud. JESUS knows I am a very shy person. He would tell me to tell them all that they did not have to believe in Him, but what I was doing to them (which was going directly to the part of their body that had pain) was surfacing their pain without touching them and telling them, "In the name of JESUS." That was all JESUS had me say, "In the name of JESUS." I would say that over and over for less than a minute and they were healed. Healing miracles are instant in the name of JESUS.

I told you I witnessed fish scales the size of 1-millimeter fly off Estella's eyes (my Mom) and gave her perfect vision. JESUS told me "fish scales' as I watch them spit out of her eyes. 15 years later, I read about the "scales" being removed from
Saint Paul's eyes. Amazing the things JESUS had me do. Amazing. There is much to say but really, the truth is salvation for all from our Lord JESUS.

JESUS healed all, "And the whole multitude sought to touch Him, for powers went out from Him and healed them all." All sinners were healed. None were Christians when JESUS healed them all. JESUS had not yet shed His blood to save us back in the days before His death. That is why Christianity is not a religion. It is salvation. The Holy Bible is spiritual.

JESUS heals all today, even non-Christians. I have witnessed many modern day miracles JESUS has done. Each time is was like I was in a trance when JESUS used me to approach certain people. I walked away each time knowing our Lord JESUS healed them. GOD wants no one to suffer. JESUS is the healer. You can go directly to JESUS to be healed. Sin is no longer the issue of not being healed, it is doubt, and so have faith in JESUS. Grace is upon us all. Heaven and Earth will pass away; the Holy Bible tells us there will be a new Heaven and a new Earth, new organization by GOD.

You must be a believer and saved, born-again. Respond to the Gospel message JESUS has said Himself, [84]"that which is born of the flesh is flesh, and that which is born of the Spirit is Spirit. So Do not be surprised when I (JESUS) say you must be born again." JESUS said, "Truly, truly, I tell you, no one can see the Kingdom of GOD unless he is born again." You must be born again to enter the Kingdom of GOD.

---

[84] John 3:3-7

If you stay in the flesh you are either responding to GOD rebelliously or a religious response to GOD. Christianity is not a religion and being born again is spiritual.

Do not be ignorant to the truth of how one can enter the Kingdom of GOD. Doing what you think is right or thinking Karma (Karma is a stupid new wave word, the Golden Rule is what is in the Gospel)…will not allow you to enter the Kingdom of GOD. You cannot merit (a quality of being good or worthy of deserving praise or a reward) GOD'S favor. The Gospel is not karma. Again, the Gospel of GOD is not karma. The devil wants you to think karma will get you into the next life of eternity with GOD in His Kingdom, which is untrue. Karma is not repent and belief in JESUS. Karma is not the message from JESUS.

Be [85]born of the Spirit is New Covenant. [86]JESUS CHRIST promises that if the believer will commit himself to accepting His blood as the Everlasting Covenant and have total dependence on the [87]Grace of JESUS CHRIST sacrifice for you along with His promise to change your life is New Covenant. JESUS' blood of the Everlasting Covenant, the New Covenant is what washes away our sins, and His promise to write His laws in our hearts and in our minds is what empowers us to live a godly life.

This is the promise made by JESUS: [88]" I will put my laws in their minds and write it on their hearts." [89]We are all born in sin. [90]"You were dead in your sins and because you're sinful nature was not yet cut away. Then God made you alive with Christ, for he forgave all our sins.

---

[85] John 3:5

[86] Hebrews 9: 12-14; Hebrews 13:11-12; Romans 3:25; Ephesians 1:7

[87] Galatians 6:18; Revelation 22:21; 2 Timothy 2:1; Philippians 1:2

[88] Jeremiah 31:33; Hebrews 10:16; Ephesians 2:5

[89] Psalms 51:5; Romans 5:12-19

He (GOD The Father) canceled the record of the charges against us and took it away by nailing it to the cross." GOD nailed the Ten Commandments to the cross at the crucifixion of JESUS.

Just because you go to a Church that may state "New Covenant" church, you may still be living under the Old Covenant if you think you live a good life under the law of karma. No. That is still living under the Old Covenant way and thinking as they did thousands of years ago.
You must be converted into the New Covenant. This is a serious matter. There exist lost Old Covenant Christians. Has nothing to do with the Ten Commandments but how you are responding to GOD in Faith. It is total submission to GOD who will write His laws in our hearts and in our minds.

The New Covenant is a transformation in your life. Do you love GOD? If you love GOD, then allow Him to write His laws in our hearts and in our minds. Sincerely seek and trust in GOD.

Paul truthfully states,[91]"He (JESUS) has enabled us to be ministers of His New Covenant. This is a covenant not of written laws, but of the Spirit. The old written covenant ends in death; but under the New Covenant, the Spirit gives life. The old way, with laws etched in stone (Ten Commandments), came with glory, so that the Israelites could not bear to look at Moses' face. For his face shone with the glory of GOD, even though brightness was already fading away. Shouldn't we expect far greater glory under the new way, now that the Holy Spirit is giving life? If the old way, which brings condemnation, was glorious, how much glorious is the new way; which makes us right with GOD!"

---

[90] Colossians 2:13; Ephesians 2:1

[91] 2 Corinthians 3:6-9

The New Covenant is righteousness and life eternal. Do not reject the Gospel of GOD and Do not have a legalistic view of it either. Have faith and embrace the Gospel. There is only one life, one Gospel, one Truth in which to determine your destiny.

It is through JESUS CHRIST we enter into the New Covenant. Come to the place and conviction by GOD that you ask GOD to help you. Ask JESUS to enter your life and take over your life. The Spirit of GOD brings the new birth into your life. There will be a conversion in you.

Trust in GOD and in His promises. Truth. JESUS will save you. Do not go the other direction. Go towards JESUS. The Gospel is total, 100% faith in JESUS CHRIST. Be certain that you are going to the Kingdom of GOD when you die. I am witness to the Holy Bible is true and GOD is real and JESUS lives. There really is eternal life after death. Again, you have two choices. Either Heaven or hell is your only two choices. Both are eternal living, never to end.

You are in charge of your demise, your immortality home eternal. When you die you live again, but your location is either in hell or in the Kingdom of GOD. There is life after death. Focus on eternal life with our Lord GOD.
The devil wants either you to believe there is no life after death or all go into a blissful place. The devil wants all to go to hell were his home has been established by, Our Creator, GOD. Follow JESUS CHRIST and live in His Kingdom. You can know truth be simply asking JESUS.

No one leaves Earth without a final spiritual destiny already established by your freewill. JESUS said in His word, the Holy Bible,[92]"It is appointed to everyone of us, once to die." Know this fact, everyone in hell is a believer (believer in JESUS CHRIST), but by then it is too late to repent and believe in JESUS.

---

[92] Hebrews 9:27

The wisest man ever created by GOD, King Solomon makes clear,[93] "It is the same for all. There is one fate for the righteous and for the wicked; for the good, for the clean and for the unclean; for the man who offers a sacrifice and for the one who does not sacrifice. As the good man is, so is the sinner; as the swearer is, so is the one who is afraid to swear. This is an evil in all that is done under the sun, that there is one fate for all men."

---

[93] Ecclesiastes 9:1-12

8

ARE YOU SURE, YOU ARE GOING TO THE KINGDOM OF GOD? FEDERAL PRISON WITH FAITH IN JESUS

JESUS tells us that death is one fate for all of us, but two fates after death, Glory with JESUS or hell with evil and all that is condemned. Choose life eternal in the Kingdom of GOD. If you do not choose JESUS, then you have chosen satan and all evil with him and all condemnation. Do not become a believer when it is too late and you are in the pit, in hell, in gehenna eternal. Choose your final destination to be in the Kingdom of GOD and not hell.

JESUS spoke more about hell in the Holy BIBLE. JESUS told us that hell is an actual location, and real place. Hell, also called gehenna is not a state of mind. If you choose hell, you are never coming out. It is a final destination for non-believers that JESUS is Our Lord, Our Savior, Our GOD. Save yourself and go to the other final destination, the Kingdom of GOD. JESUS said non-believers, "these will go away into eternal punishment, but the righteous (the believers in JESUS) into eternal life."

There are two real locations, hell or heaven (Kingdom of GOD). JESUS told us in the Holy Bible that if you choose hell out of free will, it is a place of agony indescribable. [94]Eternal torment: JESUS tells us "the fire is not quenched," not put out in hell.

---

[94] Mark 9:48; Revelation 14:10

Choose eternal joyful life, the Kingdom of GOD. We are all foretold that hell is "outer darkness." We are foretold that hell is a place[95] "there will be weeping and gnashing of teeth." Continuous suffering is hell.

Never ending torment is hell. Separation from GOD is hell. Do not believe the devil or people who claim that the 'lake of fire' is for a moment. JESUS said it is "eternal." Non-believers will suffer forever and ever. For non-believers JESUS said, "these will go away into eternal punishment, but the righteous (believers in JESUS CHRIST) into eternal life."

Hell is eternal and Heaven is eternal. Hell is everlasting torment and Heaven is eternal comfort. Trust in JESUS CHRIST. Are you a Christian who has repented and become a "new creation" in JESUS CHRIST or are you thinking of yourself to be a Christian simply because you go to church and do good works.

You must have faith in JESUS. You must humble yourself. I am writing this in plain easy to read language as JESUS instructed me to. You must repent of your sins and allow JESUS to be your Lord; acknowledge that JESUS is the Son of GOD; JESUS was crucified for the remissions of our sins, the entire sins of the world; JESUS died and rose again (He defeated death); believe in JESUS.

---

[95] Matthew 13:10

Repentance is changing your mind towards sins and towards GOD. Again, save yourself by saying these words and truly by faith accepting JESUS as the Son of GOD. Speak,

JESUS I believe you are the Son of GOD. I believe You are GOD in the flesh sent by GOD the Father. I believe You gave your life freely and laid it down at the cross where You where crucified for our sins. You JESUS took my place of judgment. You died for the remission of my sins and took my judgment upon yourself. You are my Lord and Savior and my GOD. JESUS, enter my heart and anew my spirit. I believe JESUS rose again in fulfillment of the Holy Scriptures. I believe JESUS is resurrected and is seated at the right hand of our Heavenly Father GOD. If you have said these words to GOD then you have chosen to let JESUS enter you and have willfully chosen eternal life with GOD.

Salvation is mine and salvation can be yours too. JESUS freely gives us salvation. This is the spirit of faith. Faith in JESUS is your path to salvation. Believe it and speak it be saved eternally. With the heart believe unto righteousness and with the mouth confess into salvation. Possess the spirit of faith in JESUS.

Salvation is a gift from GOD, who brought us back to himself through Christ. GOD has given us this task of, reconciling people to him. For GOD was in Christ, reconciling the world to Himself, no longer counting people's sins against us who believe in Him. He gave us this wonderful message of reconciliation. So we are Christ's ambassadors; GOD is making his appeal through us. We speak for Christ when we plead, "Come back to GOD!"

For GOD made Christ, who never sinned, to be the offering for our sin, so that we could be made right with GOD through Christ." The Kingdom of GOD is beyond description. JESUS tells us there are mansions for believers in His Father's house; [96]"In my Father's house are many mansions: if it were not so, I would have told you. I go to prepare a place for you (believers in JESUS). "Then I saw a new heaven and a new earth, for the first heaven and the first earth had passed away, and the sea was no more. And I saw the holy city, new Jerusalem, coming down out of heaven from GOD, prepared as a bride adorned for her husband. And I heard a loud voice from the throne saying, "Behold, the dwelling place of GOD is with man. He will dwell with them, and they will be his people, and GOD himself will be with them as their GOD. He will wipe away every tear from their eyes, and death shall be no more, neither shall there be mourning, nor crying, nor pain anymore, for the former things have passed away." And He who was seated on the throne said, "Behold, I am making all things new."

Also He said, "Write this down, for these words are trustworthy and true." ...Amen, so be it. This world will die and go away and replaced by GOD.

[97]Hell was made for satan and his followers, but enlarged for those people who reject the Love of GOD, the Love of JESUS who is GOD. Son of GOD is JESUS. Eternal destination is, made by you, not GOD. GOD so loved the world. GOD chose everyone in the world. Everyone has free will to chose Heaven, the Kingdom Of GOD or hell. Voluntarily choose GOD, JESUS.

---

[96] John 14:2

[97] Matthew 25:41; Revelation 20:10

I plead with you, do not become a believer in JESUS after it's too late and you are in hell, humbled by your own choice. GOD tells us, He sent His only Son, JESUS. Listen and pay attention to GOD. Think about the end of you on earth and beginning of your eternal destination. GOD sent His Son JESUS so that no one would have to go to hell. JESUS paid the price for every person to choose the Kingdom of GOD as a final place to live spiritually. Through JESUS blood, all sins were forgiven.

Understand that satan wants you to think there is no hell. Come to repentance so you do not perish to hell eternal. JESUS is a loving GOD. Do not join lucifer (satan) and one-third of the fallen angels in hell. GOD is love. The evil angels rejected GODS love, rebelled against GOD and cast out of GODS Kingdom forever. This all happened before any man or woman was created. JESUS said He saw[98] "satan (lucifer) fall like lightning from Heaven." Like lightning, satan was thrown to the earth. Hell was created for the devil and the angles that followed satan or were tricked by satan. They will suffer eternal. Do not join them. Do not let the devil trick you.

"Hell was prepared for the devil and his angels." They had free will and so do you. Free will to choose Heaven or hell, to choose Creator or created, to choose love or hate. Do not reject GOD and His Son JESUS. Do not hurt our GOD. You do not like rejection? Rejection hurts JESUS. Emotions were given us through JESUS. Those were His first.

---

[98] Luke 10:18

[99]The world's sin is that it refuses to believe in me. Righteousness is available because I go to the Father, and you will see me no more. Judgment will come because the ruler of this world has already been judged (satan, the devil). The devil, satan (lucifer) has been judged. The GOD The Holy Spirit gives all believers a clear and divine disclosure, making known to you all secrets and information of the facts of this world, the devil does not want you to know. Do not fear death. The devil wants you to fear death.

Remember, JESUS remitted, cancelled all our sins when he gave Himself, took ours sins and at the cross, defeated death. JESUS paid our debt and took our punishment under the law (Ten Commandments). JESUS' blood perfectly remitted and cleansed our sins.

JESUS took our infirmities, our affliction, illness, disease, sickness and weakness at the cross where He was crucified.[100]"Because GODS children are human beings--made of flesh and blood--the Son also became flesh and blood. For only as a human being could He (JESUS) die, and only by dying, could He (JESUS) break the power of the devil, who had the power of death. Only in this way could he set free all who have lived their lives as slaves to the fear of dying." Like I said previously, all creatures in hell become a believer, but it is too late to be saved and enter the Kingdom of GOD. Today, right now give your life to JESUS.

---

[99] John 16:9-11

[100] Hebrews 2:14-15

Make a decision either to go to hell or make your future in the Kingdom of GOD. It is your decision. If you choose hell and choose not to believe in JESUS at the cross, then you will be separated from GOD and all those who believe. Hell is a real place and it is all eternity. GOD loves you! GOD loves you! If you reject GODS plan of salvation of eternal life in His Kingdom, then you will go to hell. GOD has no choice but to send you to hell when you stand before Almighty GOD on judgment day. What I write is real and truth. When GOD judges you, He has no choice but to banish (divine punishment, transport) your soul to hell, if you while on earth, in flesh and blood, choose not to accept JESUS as you Savior, your Lord, your KING.

GOD has no choice but to send your soul away forever and ever into eternal separation from Him. That means to live with the liar satan and forever living in pain and sorrow. Do not reject GODS salvation. Do not reject the Gospel of CHRIST, The Holy Bible. Do not reject life by choosing death, the second death. [101]"And just as each person is destined to die once and after that comes judgment, so also CHRIST died once for all time as a sacrifice to take away the sins of many people. He will come again, not to deal with our sins, but to bring salvation to all who are eagerly waiting for him." GOD loves you!

GOD sent His Son JESUS CHRIST because He loves you. GOD sent JESUS to die in our place, wiping away the sins of this world, but you must choose salvation. Salvation is the forgiveness of all sins JESUS took and replaced with righteousness. Don't you know, JESUS freely gives us salvation? This is the spirit of faith.

---

[101] Hebrews 9:27, 28

Salvation is deliverance from sin and the consequences going to hell, which can only be brought about by faith in JESUS. Believe it and speak it to be saved eternally. GOD loves you. He sent JESUS CHRIST His Son because of His love for us all. GOD offers salvation, the cleansing of our sins. This is great love only GOD can give and has given us to choose. GOD offers forgiveness. You have to be willing to accept His words. Accept it.

Hear GODS words. JESUS loves you. GOD said through Apostle[102]Paul, "but God showed his great love for us by sending Christ to die for us while we were still sinners." Are you sure you are saved? Are you sure you are going to the Kingdom of GOD? Are you sure? JESUS loves you! Repent and follow CHRIST. Have you made a decision? What is your decision? You have two choices and they are both eternity destinations. The decision can only be made by you and not by your church, or family or spouse. You and no one else can only make the decision.

GOD sent His Son JESUS to our lost selves. JESUS said to both Luke and Mathew his disciples,[103]"For the Son of Man came to seek and save those who are lost." Are you lost? Are you saved? Do not just hope you are; know you are going to Heaven. Know you are forgiven. Are you going to the Kingdom of GOD? Be sure you are saved. Be sure you are going to Heaven. Be sure.[104]The Holy Bible says, "If you confess with your mouth that Jesus is Lord and believe in your heart that God raised him from the dead, you will be saved."

What is in your heart? Do you have a relationship with JESUS? The decision is to be made now. Do not wait. Time is

---

[102] Romans 5:8

[103] Luke 19:10 & Mathew 18:11

[104] Romans 10:9

not on our side. An urgent matter waits for no one. GOD reaches out to you. Take a hold of Him now. Choose JESUS. [105]" For God says, "at just the right time, I heard you. On the day of salvation, I helped you." Indeed, the "right time" is now. Today is the day of salvation." The time to choose is now. Choose GODS love by accepting CHRIST JESUS. It is your decision to make.

If you wait and die without being saved, the decision will be made for you and it will be eternal damnation, forever in pain and sorrow with the devil. Understand your future and your only two choices. Understand JESUS gave you a choice to wipe away your sins and forgiveness that leads to salvation and eternal fellowship with GOD as His child. Do you understand?

Call on GOD. Choose His plan of salvation. Be free of the devil. Free from hell. Can you say you are free? Pray, repent and live for CHRIST. Pray to GOD these words, "dear GOD, I am a sinner and I am sorry for my sins. Forgive me GOD. I believe JESUS CHRIST is Your Son, took my sins to the cross, and died in my place by shedding His blood for me. I believe You raised Him on the 3rd day to life. I invite JESUS into my heart and trust Him as my Savior. I will follow Him as the Lord of my life forever. IN THE NAME OF JESUS, I pray to you GOD. Amen, Amen, & Amen. If you prayed the above prayer, you are saved and I will see you in the Kingdom of GOD. Amen brothers and sisters, Amen.
We are children of the most High GOD. Ask GOD to open all the right doors for you and to close and lock all the wrong doors. Ask GOD to bring believers into your life and to weed out the ones He chooses not to bring into your life. GOD is love and that is what we all strive for. Ask GOD to help you fulfill the plan He has laid out for you. Pray to GOD.

---

[105] 2 Corinthians 6:2

If you think you do not know how to pray, GOD will show and tell you how. GOD told me to pray in, through JESUS, and in JESUS' name. Keep prayers simple. JESUS knows what you need before you ask. GOD once had me pray in front of a congregation, which stunned me, but felt righteous. Ask GOD to infill you with sensitive spiritual ears and eyes. Ask GOD to help you resist temptations of evil. Realize that there is always going to be evil on earth. Realize that JESUS will be coming back soon. Realize that JESUS is going to wipe out all the evil, with one breath.

It took almost half a century to save me from the reality of hell bound. It has taken others less than a decade to be saved. GOD gives us free will to choose. Some believers open doors to demons not even knowing they have opened that door. Porn is a door opener for demons to enter. Excessive beer, wine, and liquor are another demonic passage, keeping you bondage. If this is you, as it was I briefly, find your way to JESUS or back to JESUS.

In 2013 I was transforming spiritually and I told GOD with all that I am, I want to be a better person, to stop lying and deceitful. To do your will no matter what the cost is. In the blink of an eye, I found myself in County jail for seven months. Federal detainer held me in county jail awaiting sentencing, then prison until April 2014, pre-release until March 2015.

The entire time I was in GODS Grace. GOD was with me. I planted seeds everywhere I went. Around whomever I met. From jailers to inmates to counselors including ministers, I planted GODS seeds through and in JESUS. I was and am a JESUS girl. The entire time I meditated in the Lord GOD. Every move I made I asked GOD to have His hand on it.

The beginning of my incarceration started when FBI agent knocked on my door and soon after I was indicted for theft of government money. Simply, I had Medicaid pay for my surgeries in 2008 and 2013.

The government was able to make a case against me with a settlement I received in 2007. Once again, that is a separate worldly factual story. I initially tried to represent myself because of all the evil around me. The magistrate told me to get an attorney. The US District Courts tried to give me and had issued me a Federal public defender that GOD told me was evil. He explained that in Federal Court, sentencing is not reduced. I was being sentenced on three counts totaling 25 years in Federal prison. I told the magistrate that GOD was in control. He quickly told me that GOD was not going to sit with me in jail. On the drive home with my present mother-in-law, I began to cry profusely. I said that I was in over my head. I looked in the phone book repeatedly and could not find one Federal attorney in Flathead County.

I called my beautiful husband Steve and could hardly speak. All of a sudden, I felt the presence of GOD who told me HE would deliver me. I went from hysteric to beyond calm. I was joyful. I immediately told my mother-in-law what GOD said to me and called my husband and told him too. When I got home, GOD told me to look in the phone book for an attorney. I told him I already did and there is not one in there or Flathead County. I looked again and three big ads of the same Federal attorney, a former Federal prosecutor in Texas where I am originally from was before my eyes. GOD said, call him. I thought to myself, no one answering my call since it was past 6pm. Well the attorney answered the phone and scheduled me to see him at 9am the next morning. I told my husband that GOD said HE would deliver me. I called my former spouse and told him what had happened.

The next morning at 8:55 am, he called me and said there was a check at the Bank for $5,000 for counsel. I told the Federal attorney that GOD was in control and had sent me to him. He needed exactly $5,000 to handle the entire case. Satan and his fallen angels caused me much pain and hurdles throughout the process.

There was given me a plea agreement. I sign it without reading it. My faith in GOD and HIS word to deliver me swiftly was my sight. After signing it, it said I would do 10 years in Federal prison in exchange for dropping two of the three indictments. Wow! O.KKKKK.

I went to jail. I sat seven months in county jail before the Feds would take me to prison. I received 8 months in prison and had already sat 7 months in county jail on a Federal Detainer (23 hour lock down). The whole punishment took nearly two years of incarceration and 7 months pre-release before I would return to my home, my husband and my dog, Daisy May. Daisy died a month ago. I told her about JESUS.

GOD said to tell every creature that breathes about Him. She was a JESUS dog. The Montana legal system is getting better because the good ole boys are dead or too old to have any power. The blood money they leave behind are wasting by their family who love money and so much the power.

Quatmann and Quatmann, a law firm in Whitefish knows exactly what I speak of. Our Supreme Court Justices are just as bad. Brian Morris, no relation is an unlawful justice. Patricia Cottor is totaling law abiding constitutional and statue direct justice. She is the best of the best.

Montanans, beware of the church formerly "Scull Church" – [106]"wolves dressed in sheep clothing."

Canvas Church is a Holy place for children and families to be saved. The Lead Pastor Kevin Geer is the best in Kalispell, Montana and in this country, next to my Pastor Frank Vargas.

---

[106] Matthew 7:15

I firmly believe that every pause in life, the five minutes it took for me to recover my driver's license from you was by GOD for divine reason." That reason is to plant or water seeds of JESUS as our GOD. She apologized and I said to her, "Do not worry GOD is in control. Do not let the devil plant, "seeds of doubt" JESUS told me. Whether I literally stumble, or pause for someone, GOD has chosen a path for my good. A moment in time defines a destiny. Let GOD choose your destiny.

Become a JESUS boy or JESUS girl. Let them (GOD, JESUS and the HOLY SPIRIT) take control of your life now and eternal. Place no confidence in your flesh. Put all confidence in JESUS CHRIST. Be under Grace. Grow in the Grace of GOD once you are saved. Once you have freely accepted JESUS CHRIST as our savior, Son of GOD.

When you are saved you, speak from your heart. Your actions are a reflection of your heart. When you are saved your work of faith, your patience of hope and your labor of love is under the Grace of GOD. You are righteous by faith in GOD.

JESUS gave Himself to die on the cross freely. Freely He laid down His life for us. No one could take His life. At the cross JESUS, His flesh not His Divine Spirit took our condemnation. JESUS bore our sins past, present and future at the cross.

We are now "dead to sins."[107]"In the same way, count yourselves dead to sin but alive to GOD in CHRIST JESUS." JESUS never bore our sins in His Spirit.

There was no other way to save us from sin, from death, from judgment. Under Grace, we have been given mercy. JESUS is most holy. Being dead to sin, we are the righteousness in CHRIST JESUS. By JESUS' death, we are dead to sin, since we are new creations in CHRIST JESUS.

---

[107] Romans 6:11

We rest in JESUS. We no longer are under the power of sin. Confess, "I am the righteousness of GOD in CHRIST". You are righteous before GOD and equal with the same standing as all pastors, priest and even the pope. GOD loves you just as much as GOD loves those who are saved.

I recently asked the Lord about generational curse, mainly because my Dad was a child molester and wife beater. After his death, I later found out that his older brother had molested his children too. I knew about generational curses from the old testament in which GOD said to them through Moses on Mount Sinai,[108]"The Lord is longsuffering, and of great mercy, forgiving iniquity and transgression, and by no means clearing the guilty, visiting the iniquity of the fathers upon the children unto the third and forth generation."

Our GOD, [109]"JESUS CHRIST is the same yesterday and today and forever." Are you in pain? Are you suffering? Are you in torment? Are you lost and confused? Cry out to JESUS.

There were evil sexual demons/spirits that lived in our house preying and tormenting all of us. I did not know then, but I do now, the power in the name of JESUS. One day I will see them and judge them to the pit. Those saved as "new creation in CHRIST, old things have passed away," includes every generational curse. All things have become new. Generational curse was before Grace saved us believers. However, generational curse exist for non-believers and only rebuked through faith in JESUS. Believers have the power of JESUS to rebuke evil. Those outside JESUS CHRIST, the generational curse is real. Those in CHRIST, have no generational curse.

---

[108] Psalm 145:8; Numbers 14:18; Exodus 34:6

[109] Hebrews 13:8

9

THE GRACEFUL FIRST LADY MELANIA TRUMP REPENT AND BELIEVE IN JESUS

Dad was very good to me, but he was with sisters and cousins and I am sure other victim's. His Dad was a child molester too. He repented and always believed in JESUS, but repentance saved my Dad. Although older sister forgave him, the forgiveness was for her salvation, not his. That is how forgiveness works. It is for the person who is filled with anger and hurt, not for the person they are angry.

Dad will be in the Kingdom of GOD. Understand you believers in JESUS; you must repent to be in the Kingdom of GOD. I love and forgive the way my siblings have hurt, and shunned me, but my heart to forgive them is so JESUS will not judge me.[110]"Forgive, and you will be forgiven." Whether they care or not is between them and JESUS. I worry for my love for JESUS. Everyone including family who I have hurt I ask for your forgiveness.

Oh, happy birthday J.D., I have tried mailing you and did try texting you a birthday wish, but you blocked my number although JESUS is the one who gave me your cell number off a Refugio, Texas hurricane blog. I asked JESUS not to hold your hurting me against you, but I do ask you grow in the LORD GOD JESUS. It hurts JESUS to see my feelings hurt, but in reality it hurts me to see JESUS hurt. JESUS gave us these emotions, thus He possessed them before we were created.

---

[110] Luke 6:37

Through the shedding of JESUS' blood, satan and his followers are defeated. Amen. Thank you LORD JESUS. All our past, present and future sins are forgiven by JESUS and gone by the precious blood of JESUS. Hallelujah! Thank you in JESUS' name. Amen.

Rest in JESUS and be protected by His power, His love, His Grace. When you take Communion, believe JESUS bore our diseases, carried our pain and when you take Communion you are healed physically from what ails you.

Believe. Believe. Believe. Recognize that the LORD'S Supper heals, as you partake in the Holy Communion you will begin to feel healing. The spirit of GOD gives life. Follow the spirit of GOD. Your attitude before you partake in the LORD'S Supper, the Holy Communion is realizing that you have to examine yourself first. You have to be right with JESUS, who is GOD.

I am in fellowship with CHRIST JESUS. JESUS is the Son of GOD. He is GOD. We are creatures of GOD. GOD is our Creator. We have two choices. We can choose to live with our LORD JESUS or we can choose live without. The first choice leads to eternal life. The second choice leads to eternal darkness. JESUS does not disappear or nonexistent because there are atheist. We are not talking about blind faith. Intelligent faith exists. Believe and speak of your faith. We receive righteousness by believing in JESUS. The greatest blessing we can receive is salvation. Forgiveness of all sins JESUS took and replaced with righteousness. With the heart believe unto righteousness and with the mouth confess into salvation. Possess the spirit of faith in JESUS. Amen, so be it.

You can be a good church member and still not be saved. I believed in JESUS but I did not repent. When I truly repented, then my eyes were opened to Grace. GOD led me to GOD. JESUS led me to GOD. No one witnessed to me. It was JESUS who told me He is CHRIST and was CHRIST before coming as a Man. JESUS told me and showed me many truths before I read it in the Holy Bible. JESUS CHRIST revealed parts of the gospel to me. JESUS would tell me things in single words or as I mentioned prior, "daughter,[111]no one called my name," the longest sentenced with me. I did not know what Grace meant.

In 2012 when I started Holy Bible studies, I asked everyone, "What is this Grace." I would ask, "What does this Grace feel like?" I had no clue what this "Grace" was or meant, even as a believer in JESUS. Roman Catholic churches and school did not teach me what "Grace," meant or how to enter the Kingdom of GOD.

Instead, I verified the Vatican and all Roman Catholic churches work to put money into the Popes and his cohorts are just an institution making money for greed. A moneymaking machine filled with evil. They will all meet JESUS soon.

JESUS told me the rapture is within 14 years from my vision in the spirit. Then the anti CHRIST will reveal his evil self from the Middle East and everyone will think he is JESUS but will be fooled by his pretend miracles. Dumb statues talking aloud to people who will think this must be JESUS or of good. Do not worship this false anti CHRIST and his false prophet. Do not take his mark upon your hand or head to buy food.

---

[111] Psalms 55:16

It is better to die than to go to hell for a piece of bread. The anti CHRIST will fall at the hands of JESUS. I write this book to let all know the rapture is coming soon (within 14 years) followed by the rise and fall of the anti CHRIST. (May 2032, an important date). I am not the only one JESUS told this to, many believers have been told and are warning non-believers and believers who are not born again. There is a difference between believing in JESUS and being born-again. You must be born again to enter the Kingdom of GOD, and I don't mean a water baptism but a spiritual baptism.

Know when Grace is upon you, you tend to look back into your past and you see Grace was there all along. Where there is much sinning Grace abounds.[112] "Well then, should we keep on sinning so that GOD can show us more and more of His wonderful Grace? Of course not! Since we have died to sin, how can we continue to live in it? Or have you forgotten that when we were joined with CHRIST JESUS in baptism, we joined Him (JESUS) in His death? For we died and were buried with JESUS CHRIST by baptism. And just as JESUS CHRIST was raised from the dead by the glorious power of the Father GOD, now we also may live new lives."

The Lord JESUS waits for you to acknowledge Him and the love about Him. JESUS waits for the day you make a conscience effort not to sin. Regret your sins aloud to JESUS, and ask Him to take over. Believers' right with LORD JESUS will be blessed with healing while taking the LORD'S Supper.

Thank JESUS for defeating the devil. Have faith in our LORD, our Savior JESUS. It was one of GOD'S angel who told Joseph, "for He will save His people from their sins." We are His people and He is our GOD. "So I want you to know that no one speaking by the Spirit of GOD will curse JESUS, and no one can say JESUS is LORD, except by the Holy Spirit."

---

[112] Romans 6:1-13

Before GOD created man, He created angels. There are Holy angels that are spiritual beings and like us, have free will. You don't have to be without knowledge of truth. JESUS is Truth. An election of Jews GOD did reveal to them that JESUS is HIS Son, by Faith they see. Jews will remain spiritual blind until the fullness of the Gentiles (anyone who is not Jewish), until the last Gentile has been told of JESUS CHRIST and given his life over to JESUS-born again.

Choose eternal life with JESUS. GODISJESUSLIVES. Don't choose eternal life in utter darkness where you shall suffer forever and ever eternal. Divorce yourself from this world. Be in the world and not of the world. Horror is on the Earth. The tribulation will be the final 7 years and never has there been or ever again, the horror that is upon this earth. We are approaching the final years here on earth. Look around. See all the evilness, wickedness we humans are doing upon one another.

We are under a New Testament established through JESUS. We are under a New Covenant through the blood of JESUS CHRIST. The blood of JESUS CHRIST cleansed sin. The blood of sacrificed animals covered sins under the Old Testament. GOD'S children were under the law written in stone by GOD. GOD gave us JESUS who laid His life down freely to cover our sins with His divine blood. Sin ended at the cross. JESUS is our substitute. GOD sees us as righteous. GOD sees us as He sees JESUS. Our sins have been cleansed by, the blood of JESUS. In CHRIST JESUS, cleanse you of sins. We are three part being, spirit, soul and body & mind, as GOD is, GOD the Father, GOD the Son, and GOD the Holy Spirit. The GODHEAD is three in one, as we are three in one.

Have you ever wondered how it is that you can speak to yourself in your mind? Have you ever wondered what makes the heart beat continuously? Knowing the Truth sets you free. Free to love GOD. Free to have the peace of GOD that surpasses all understanding. Please, read the gospel. Save yourself. Choose life. Who doesn't like Free? Salvation is Free!

GOD gave His Son two thousand years ago as a sacrifice to set us free. In all your ways acknowledge Him, and He shall direct your paths." JESUS said, "If anyone desires to come after Me, let him deny himself, and take up his cross daily, and follow Me. For whoever desires to save his own life will lose it, but whoever loses his life for My sake will save it. For what profit is it to a man if he gains the whole world, and is himself destroyed or lost? For whoever is ashamed of Me and My words, of him the Son of Man (JESUS) will be ashamed when He comes in His own glory, and in His Father's, and of the holy angels." GODISJESUSLIVES.

JESUS called Himself Son of Man. He had to come to us in the form of a Man, in the flesh. We must consent to placing all our worries on JESUS. GOD gives us freewill to choose our destiny. Repent by allowing JESUS to live in you and you in Him. The peace you will have by resting in JESUS will place a light of Glory around you that no evil can penetrate. JESUS is compassion. He waits for you. Once you have chosen to accept Christ JESUS, His salvation is irrevocable.

GOD'S salvation is forever lasting. We are born sinners. Repent from self-righteousness. GOD gives you rest from all the troubles of this world. Consent to be loved and rest on the stronger shoulder's of our Lord, JESUS. Receive the gift of righteousness in JESUS. When saved, born again, all sins are removed. The only authority we have is the word of GOD. The Gospel of the Kingdom of GOD (Holy Bible) speaks out all you need to know. Know what the Lord JESUS has to say by reading the gospel. I was hesitant knowing in the back of my mind that my life would change. It was life changing. It is fulfillment. True life is fulfillment.

Be united with JESUS and not what this world has to offer. Every person who chose not to believe GOD when He said JESUS is His Son will proceed to the "second death." The "second death," you are thrown into hell forever and ever.

Again, faith in JESUS is accepting JESUS as the Son of GOD. Say, JESUS, I believe you are the Son of GOD. I believe You are GOD in the flesh sent by GOD the Father. I believe You gave your life freely and laid it down at the cross where You where crucified for our sins. You JESUS took our place of judgment, died for the remission of my sins, and took my judgment upon yourself. I believe JESUS is my Lord and Savior and my GOD. I believe JESUS rose again in fulfillment of the Holy Scriptures. I believe JESUS is resurrected and is seated at the right hand of our Heavenly Father GOD. GOD sent His Son JESUS to take our sins. All we have to do is accept that by faith, complete trust in JESUS. Convert to a personal faith in CHRIST JESUS. JESUS does not want to be separated from His Children so choose LIFE Eternal.

Choose salvation, deliverance from sin and its consequences of hell, by faith in JESUS. You do not have to work for salvation. Simply accept by GODS Grace we are saved. Grace is not a created substance but the love and mercy given to us all by GOD. We cannot earn Grace. GOD desires all to be saved by His Grace.

In the Christian faith, GOD does all for us. Christianity is not a religion where you have to do something for GOD. GOD gave us His Son as a sacrifice for our sins. Grace is the love of GOD. JESUS died for us. We do not have to die for Him. Confess your personal sins directly to GOD through JESUS. Pray to GOD through JESUS. Stand and believe in JESUS. Live in JESUS. The Holy Spirit of GOD will guide you. Pray for guidance. Prayer works. Prayer is addressing GOD to a solemn request for help or giving thanks to Him. GOD hears all your prayers. Pray in the name of JESUS. Give in the name of JESUS. Live in the name of JESUS. Know biblical truth.

Stand for biblical truth. Invite CHRIST JESUS into your heart and into your life. Find your way through JESUS CHRIST if you are lost. I am witness to the fact that I saw JESUS and heard GOD.
Don't you know, Christianity is not a religion? I am a Christian saved by Grace. The most important book in the universe is to GODS Word, the gospel. The Holy Bible (Gospel of the Kingdom of GOD) was written by, GOD Almighty. No man or creature of GOD could have written the Holy Bible unless under the Holy Spirit of GOD. Grace produces power of GOD. There is power in the name of JESUS. There is no condemnation when you are under Grace, nor can sin rule your life.

The truth these present days is the Grace of JESUS saves us. Through the blood of JESUS, we are saved. Read the gospel and research for yourself what the scriptures say. Love fulfills the law. Under Grace is love for JESUS. The love of GOD is why GOD came in the form of a man, JESUS. When JESUS appears in your life, feel and embrace the love he has for you. JESUS is holy and loves you wholly. Understand Grace. Grace is not a popularity teaching- it is JESUS. Grace is the Glory of GOD that is within you and around you. Be in the sphere of GODS glorious light. The divine spirit of GOD is all around. Receive the favor of GOD.

Evil and demons serve lucifer (satan) on Earth "So I want you to know that no one speaking by the Spirit of GOD will curse JESUS, and no one can say JESUS is Lord, except by the Holy Spirit." Before GOD created man, He created angels. There are Holy angels that are spiritual beings and like us, have free will. The Holy Bible, the Gospel is written about JESUS.

The devil (satan) took 1/3 of the created angels of GOD and longer serve GOD. The demons are not the evil fallen angels locked up until Armageddon. Both serve satan the devil and spend all their time trying to destroy GOD'S creation. The demons disguise themselves as the Holy angels of GOD, as people already decease, as anyone and try to deceive all of us so that we stray away from GOD and truth. If you see or hear a spirit or person (false prophet) claiming to be good or disguised as a loved one asleep (has died) you can test that spirit to see if he is from GOD.

There are no UFOs. I believe people when they say they were abducted or saw a UFO, but those entities are demons or the devil in disguise. They can disguise themselves to play any role to trick us humans. Faith in JESUS makes demons try harder to bring us believers down to hell-separation from GOD. Demons really don't care about the unbelievers because they are already in hell. Pull yourself out while you are still able to breathe.

Obama has a chance to repent. To be born again. He is not the anti CHRIST. If anyone thinks or know who it may be then they have been left behind. Fact: The rapture takes up all the JESUS boys and girls-believers and leaves behind the non-believer's in JESUS. We can't be here when the false prophet, the false JESUS called the anti CHRIST, and the false prophet
are given power for 7 years by JESUS, because all we would have to say is the name of JESUS with our faith so strong they have no control over us, but we do them.

Some Leaders, Kings and Rulers have chosen to go against their Creator JESUS. These people have the spirit of the anti CHRIST, which you heard is coming into the world and indeed already here." The world government and appearance of the anti CHRIST is near future. Most people in these 50 states don't even know what I am talking about. Most people choose to remain ignorant. You don't have to be ignorant of these truths.

JESUS is King of Heaven and Earth, of all. The demons and satan (lucifer) will attempt to draw us away from the truth and from our faith. The devil will send false teachers and prophets. There are many anti CHRIST people and evil spirits here with us trying to make us stumble and fall with them into hell eternal, and I mean eternal and inferno. GOD said of our sins and lawless deeds, [113] "I will remember no more." GOD saved us with Grace and under Grace the law is in our hearts.

Being a JESUS girl I no longer commit adultery, or steal. Thank You JESUS for Your unmerited favorable blessings. Your timing GOD Is perfect and beyond our selfish desire. In Your name JESUS, I pray to Father GOD I always remain humbled.

Don't be misled with religion. GOD gave us His Son JESUS two thousand years ago to set us free of the bondage of hell, where we were all headed and rightfully so. [114] "It is of the LORD'S mercies that we are not consumed, because His compassions fail not," GOD'S mercies are "new every morning: great is thy faithfulness."

---

[113] Hebrews 8:12

[114] Lamentations 3:22

"Trust in the LORD (JESUS) with all your heart; and lean not unto your own understanding. You cannot say He is a prophet and not believe what GOD'S prophet is proclaiming. Calling yourself, a Christian is following JESUS with your whole heart and praying to and through Him to GOD the Father.

There is no one else that can intercede for us but JESUS. JESUS says to believe in Him 5 times in the Holy Bible, the Gospel, to follow Him. You cannot lust for the things of the world and follow JESUS at the same time. The love for money is evil, but money is not evil. You can be a billionaire and follow JESUS. You just can't idolize money. GOD blesses those financially if He so wishes to. Followers of JESUS are devoted to Him. Following JESUS cost you nothing, but everything to gain. Give JESUS all access of your life.

Melania Trump is the most precious First Lady this Country will ever know. JESUS placed her there. She is a JESUS girl doing His Gracious work, saved by strong faith in JESUS. Her beauty lies in the inside. Favor is with both her and her husband President Donald J. Trump. Father, in Your name JESUS I pray blessings of Grace and happiness with favor upon favor for Your children Melania, Donald and their family and loved ones. Amen.

Mark Stein great man speaks logic and truth. Truly blessed by JESUS, is our beloved Kellyanne Conway a JESUS girl. Salvation is hers and her families. Father I pray in Your name JESUS continued favor and protected filled with wisdom and love for Mark, Kellyanne and their spouses and children, and all those they love and pray for. Amen.

JESUS placed Meghan Markle, Duchess of Sussex in her honorable seat. JESUS' ways are unknowable. Father, in Your your name JESUS protect and shower this princess with Grace. I pray protection and joy for Meghan, her husband and family, and all those she loves and prays for. Amen.

JESUS places His children in positions to help others to repentance and belief in Him. Why He calls them home early is not for us to ask or know, but it is all for the Glory of GOD. She is a beautiful and gracious sister in CHRIST.

I have the favor of GOD. JESUS gives undeserved favor. I am an instrument of the LORD GOD. Amen. He is my Center. His Glory surrounds me and seals me. He hold all things together, He is my center, hard to explain. JESUS Is GOD and can do whatever He wants to do whenever He chooses to do it.

He can grab this Robert Mueller by his britches and dump him in a lake right now if He so chooses so right this very minute. There is nothing whether good or evil without GOD'S approval. JESUS sees what you do in darkness. [115] "Everyone who does evil hates the light, and will not come into the light for fear that their deeds will be exposed. But whoever lives by the truth comes into the light, so that it may be seen plainly that what they have done has been done in the sight of GOD."

Mueller [116] and his company, don't you know you do your deeds in the dark? Of course you... Don't you know GOD is exposing you? He is... [117]"What you said in the dark will be heard in the daylight, and what you have whispered in the ear in the inner rooms will be proclaimed from the roofs." That is what is happening now with all the corrupt people in the USA. Even to those puppets that love and idolize money belonging to JESUS. You are trying to rob JESUS. Don't you know it is complete darkness where you and your luciferians are heading? Don't you know you can repent and believe in JESUS?

---

[115] John 3:20-21

[116] Matthew 7:20

[117] Luke 12:3

Don't you know you have little time to repent? Don't you know? You are all children of the devil.

We choose our own destiny whether destruction or peace eternal. Only JESUS knows what we have already chosen. Pray people pray. A very stupid girl once said, "enough praying we need to take action" regarding guns. She needs to repent if she wants to enter the Kingdom of GOD. Rush Limbaugh, smart as a whistle, inspiring... Good light comes off Rush, a JESUS boy. Father, in Your name JESUS I pray grace continues to shower Your son Rush, his wife and family, and those he loves and prays for. Amen.

The Savage guy whom I have never heard of until three months ago while riding with my elders were listening to 880 AM radio and I immediately did not like his put down of our President Trump because he could not see above the dust. Then his self righteous self while I accidentally heard him again, now a total of 30 minutes in my life said a '128 year old lady'.... let me correct your ignorant self to the Holy Bible and to what JESUS said to us all. [118]"Then the LORD said, "My Spirit will not put up with humans for such a long time, for they are only mortal flesh. In the future, their normal lifespan will be no more than 120 years." I love correction and I am sure your listeners would too. I know Moses lived to be 120 years.

Savage is correct about Nancy Pelosi needing to retire and perhaps has dementia and he too, a JESUS boy. Nancy repent and put JESUS before your false power and money that belongs to JESUS and cant buy you repentance.

I was listening to Rush today (June 2, 2018, still cant afford my months past due $141.00 bill to Dish Network) at

---

[118] Genesis 6:3

10:30AM (Grace is upon you Travis, [119]5 the number of GOD'S Grace is 5,5, 5, 5, 5, 5, 5,5, over again into 10:30 AM when you spoke on radio) and dear brother Travis (gay man) repent if you do not want to be separated from your loved ones, your family and especially JESUS.

JESUS is, the same yesterday, today and tomorrow and will not condone sexual immorality. Quit living for today and willfully choose to follow JESUS. You have willfully chosen to follow Lucifer militant or not. JESUS loves you as His son, but you do not love Him back. Father, I pray in Your name JESUS to break the chains of the evil spirit of sexual immorality binding Your son Travis. Amen.

West Hollywood, [120] California is Sodamned and Gaymora (new words) will have to pay the consequences of their sexual immorality and of giving the key to that immoral mayor's office to a sexually immoral creation of GOD. Repent you believers in the flesh and blood. There are no storms in the Lake of Fire, but Stormy will have all eternity to desire one if she does not repent and turn to JESUS. John Heilman will not forget the day he chose lucifer over JESUS. Hell, separation from GOD is not only for those who do not believe in JESUS, but also for those who do believe in JESUS and have not repented.

If you think performing good works will get you into the Kingdom of GOD, you are wrong and the devil is in control of you. With faith in JESUS comes performances of good works for others, but good works does not create faith in JESUS. I repeat, we are not to judge but we are to hate sin.

---

[119] Five is the number of GOD's Grace; Multiplied by itself is Grace upon Grace. Five, GOD' S Grace is a   symbol of GODS goodness and favor toward flesh and blood and mentioned 318 times in the Holy Bible.

[120] Matthew 10:16

Father in Your Name JESUS I pray for West Hollywood to repent their continued sexual immorality and give the key to You JESUS. I pray repentance and belief in you JESUS for their flesh to escape the "Lake of Fire" eternal and for the dark chains to break away form them so they may enter Your light. Amen.

Hear my cry to all you brothers and sisters mine heading to the pit with lucifer. All you lost sheep are too much of this world when you are soon face to face with destiny. [121]"For the flesh desires what is against the Spirit, and the Spirit desires what is against the flesh; these are opposed to each other, so that you do not do what you want." "When you follow the desires of your sinful nature, the results are very clear: sexual immorality, impurity, lustful pleasures."

---

[121] Galatians 5:17

10

THE RAPTURE WITHIN 14 YEARS
ARMAGADDON SOON
JESUS IS COMING IN MY GENERATION

Believe in JESUS and produce obedience in JESUS. [122]"For sin shall no longer be your master, because you are not under the law, but under Grace." When GOD looks at the born again Christian, He no longer sees our sins. JESUS removed our sins as far as the East is from the West. The new you, the new creation in CHRIST, a child of GOD washed in the blood of JESUS. Adam died spiritually when He sinned. Death does not obliterate the spirit. We all have a spirit. Live in light, there is no darkness in GOD.

[123]"GOD is light and in Him is no darkness at all." Do not live in a constant state of where you should be and where you are capable of living. JESUS knew no sin but became sin so that we could be the righteousness of GOD in JESUS. GOD loves you and your imperfections. GOD knows all and knew each of us before we were born. You cannot hide from GOD. Walk in the light and have fellowship (a friendly association) with GOD and believers. We live in a constant state of not measuring up to GOD and its ok with GOD. Depend on GODS Grace. GOD'S power is made perfect during our time of weakness. When you are saved, GOD removes the shame from our lives. GOD removed my shame.

Do not be in fear. GOD will not reject you. Live functioning with Grace and love. Be loving and kind to others. Feel the love of GOD. The devil likes to turn your life into hurt and traumatic events.

[122] Romans 6:14

[123] 1John 1:5

The evil spirits, the devil likes to tell throw thoughts into your mind to control your circumstances. Most of the time the devil is speaking through your mind tricking you into believing the thoughts are your or of GOD. The devil is always throwing lies into our mind. The devil tries to keep us from doing what is right in GOD'S eyes.
The devil tries to control our relationship with others and with GOD. The devil does not want us going down the path GOD has lit up for us with His light of glory. The devil wants you thinking he is GODS voice. The devil wants you to think GOD does not love you. The devil wants you to think your family and friends do not love you. The devil wants you to think you do not love you. The devil is all lies. Do not let the devil take hold of your mind. Cast the devil away in the name of JESUS. Command away all those evil spirits of fear, of rejection, of condemnation in the name of JESUS. GOD says Himself He will never leave us or forsake (abandon) us.

While writing this book, I have to command the devil and demons to leave me alone in the name of JESUS all the time. JESUS is power. We have the authority given us by JESUS to command all evil spirits away from us and from others. I go further and in the name of JESUS command them into the pit, chain, bound, and gagged until judgment day. Amen.

"Since we have been united with Him (JESUS) in His death, we will also be raised to life as He was. We know that our old sinful selves were crucified with CHRIST JESUS so that sin might lose its power in our lives. We are no longer slaves to sin. For when we died with CHRIST JESUS we were set free from the power of sin. And since we died with JESUS CHRIST, we know we (believers) will also live with Him. We (believers) are sure of this because JESUS CHRIST was raised from the dead, and He will never die again. Death no longer has any power over Him. When He died, He (JESUS), He died once to break the power of sin.

But now that He lives, He lives for the glory of GOD. So you also should consider yourselves to be dead to the power of sin and alive to GOD through CHRIST JESUS." "Do not let sin control the way you live; do not give in to sinful desires. Do not let any part of your body become an instrument of evil to serve sin. Instead, give yourselves completely to GOD, for you were dead, but now you have new life. So use your whole body as an instrument to do what is right for the glory of GOD. Sin is no longer your master, for you no longer live under the requirements of the law. Instead, you live under the freedom of GODS Grace."

GOD did not give us the spirit of fear. JESUS always told us fear not. JESUS washed away the spirit of fear from me in 2001. I literally felt if leave, but could not see it. I was taking a shower and fear washed off me. JESUS washed fear out of my body. [124]I did not understand what was happening, but ten years later, my mind received knowledge and understanding. I literally felt spiritual fear washed off me and into the drainpipes.

Later that same year, I looked at the thick narrow oak door and saw JESUS from the top of His head down to the lower part of His chest. I said earlier JESUS appeared to me, therefore; I give testimony as a witness that GODISJESUSLIVES.

I could not look at Him very long. His presence was so powerful that I immediately bowed my head down. His hair was shoulder length. He wore a v cut collar neckline type apparel. He had a trimmed beard and mustache. His eyes are power. His nose was narrow. I asked the other people if they had seen JESUS too. No, they did not. I looked at the closet door again and like a movie reel JESUS showed me a bit of His walk with the wooden cross of his left shoulder and dragging behind Him on the narrow cobblestone road.

---

[124] Matthew 14:27 & Matthew 28:10

He wore a linen beige cover. He wore an ankle length light beige long sleeve linen garment while carrying the cross through the cobblestone street. I saw woman to the left of Him crying loud and reaching their arms towards Him. Their heads were cover but not their face and most wore black covers on their heads.

The narrow cobblestone road had a curve to it. The wooden cross drug about a foot behind JESUS. Soon after, I saw two tall and slender identical blonde women in blue and white long gowns with a sash around their upper waist while rejoicing. They spun round and round rejoicing. They were holy angels. I did not see whether they had feet, as the heavenly gown they wore covered them completely to the ground. The identical carbon copy angels spun at the same time.

It was not until 2011 that JESUS revealed to me that the angelic looking women rejoiced because He had defeated death. I attribute that lack of spiritual growth in not reading the most lively and divine book in the whole universe, the Holy Bible. Even after seeing JESUS, I still chose to be of this world. I was still on the path to eternal damnation.

I even had supernatural occurrences all around me with knowledge and wisdom tied to JESUS, yet I did not care enough to do His calling for me specific. It had been months of imagining a vibrant white light around me to protect me from evil. I start at the tip of my head and outline my body with the light. I went around my shoulder and down my arm. I envisioned the light around each finger and back up my inner arm. Down my side, down my leg, around my toes, up my inner leg and thigh, back down the other leg, around my toes, back up my leg and side down my arm around my other fingers up my arm up my shoulder, around my head to meet the point I had begun. I told no one when I would put what I felt was GODS protection.

Fifteen years later, GOD told me it is the armor of light to cast off the works of darkness. GOD has sealed me with His name. I knew the devils and demons up high and down low surrounded me. Every morning I put on GODS Armour of light. I had sensed evil at my mother-in law's house and placed the light of protection around me. I would expand the light. I imagined it getting thicker and could feel the power. Suddenly, Larry looked at me and said, [125] "Yvonne, there is a light around you." I said to him that he saw what I had been doing for a while now but told no one. I did not want people to think I was off camber. He even confirmed that it was getting larger and larger. I knew it GOD allowed him to see it. Evil could definitely see it. I knew fifteen years ago, to put light around me to seal me with His Glory and continue to surround myself with GOD'S Glorious light.

Mother had been staying with ex-husband no.2 and me after the death of his mother. One day she told me how DJ, one of my king Doberman pup had been barking up at the ceiling when suddenly something hit him on his head causing him to yelp.

Days later she said that Husband's deceased grandmother appeared to her in the bedroom she occupied. Mom told that entity that she was dead and that evil spirit smiled and disappeared. I knew there was much evil it that home.

An evil spirit even said "Yvonne" in my ear. GOD had already removed fear from me, so it scared me not. I know now, evil is not eye level to us. Evil spirits are up high or down low, unless inside a person.

---

[125] Psalms 139:11; Psalms 97:11

Evil was all around and in the house of my former mother-in-law (Husband's Mom). She had regulatory arthritis. There was much worldly desire for her wealth. I think there was a plot to her death and to frame me for it. GOD placed us three steps ahead, of his families' worldly plots to frame me. Many, many evil plots occurred. GOD protected me and had His Angels or an Angel keep me in certain places at certain times.

The worldly people plotting evil against me did not know how I was able to know things. Never did it enter their minds that GOD was in control. That worldly true event is story that deals with evil people serving evil spirits. They all were living for power and money.

There was a time that the leader of that group was in court testifying regarding a certain matter and his eyes glowed blood red. I was not the only one witnessing that and it happened again to a girl in my same prison cell. Even on his deathbed, he asked ex-husband no.2 if he was "still married to that bitch." We had been divorced for years. My former father-in-law lived with a strong hate for me.

Harvey Weinstein it is not to late for you to repent and believe in JESUS to save yourself from the jaw of satan, lucifer. Be thankful that you still have time to save yourself. Again, save yourself by saying these words and truly by faith accepting JESUS as the Son of GOD.

I hope Charles Krauthammer and Anthony Bourdain are JESUS boys; cause hell is no gourmet dish. Apparently, demons got in Anthony's head.

No one can prepare for eternal torment. Speak out, JESUS, I believe you are the Son of GOD. I believe You are GOD in the flesh sent by GOD the Father. I believe You gave your life freely and laid it down at the cross where You where crucified for our sins. You JESUS took our place of judgment and died for the remission of my sins. You took my judgment upon yourself. I believe JESUS is my Lord and Savior and my GOD. I believe JESUS rose again in fulfillment of the Holy Scriptures. I believe JESUS resurrected and seated at the right hand of our Heavenly Father GOD.

If you are left behind after the rapture for believers, and see JESUS coming again through the clouds and have not proclaimed Him your personal Savior and Lord, you will have missed your opportunity to leave this world without experiencing Armageddon. Don't you know Armageddon is seven years of suffering with the inability to die, although you will want to die?

The resurrection is soon, [126]"for a time is coming when all who are in their graves will hear His voice and come out- those who have done what is good will rise to live (enter the Kingdom of GOD) and those who have done what is evil will rise to be condemn."

Hear the words of JESUS all you luciferians, false news and deep state (which is dark state) [127] government officials and world leaders. What good is it for someone to the gain the whole world, yet forfeit their soul?" All you luciferians are at war with GOD. Repent and believe that JESUS is LORD GOD to all.

Faith in JESUS is a spiritual trait and not obtained by site or emotion. Faith is spiritual. Faith starts by confessing with your mouth that JESUS is Lord.

---

[126] John 5:28-29

[127] Mark 8:36

Understand you luciferians you are created flesh and blood, a creature of GOD. The time for all to repent and believe in JESUS is here and now. I was called, chosen by JESUS to warn all unbelievers of the time being now. If you were to die right now, would you rise to be condemned by JESUS?

Robert Mueller and company, y'all are perfect luciferians in need of repentance and belief you are not more powerful or clever to handle defeat upon our LORD GOD JESUS. All you top level government officials who have dirty hands and run in the same circle as Clapper, Brennan, Mueller, etc., continue down your path of darkness in conspiring against President Trump and all the innocent people you have framed with false testimonies. JESUS is going to expose you all very, very, very soon.

Psalm 70 "Make haste, O GOD, to deliver me, make haste to help me, O LORD. Let them be ashamed and confounded that seek after my soul; let them be turned backward, and put to confusion, that desire my hurt. Let them be turned back for a reward of their shame that say, Aha, aha. Let all those that seek thee rejoice and be glad in thee; and let such as love thy salvation say continually, Let GOD be magnified. But I am poor and needy; make haste unto me, O GOD; thou art my help and my deliverer; O LORD make no tarrying."

Robert Mueller, stop the deception, the false witnessing before your shame is really exposed by JESUS. Right Now! You already shame the last name-Mueller.

David Petraeus is a JESUS boy and loved by JESUS. Father, in Your name JESUS I pray showers of grace, health and blessings for David and his family, and those he loves and prays for. Amen.

Not late for shameful FBI agents Strzok and Page to repent and believe. JESUS loves y'all equally. Father, in Your name JESUS I pray Your shameful children Strzok and Page repent and believe in You LORD GOD. Let salvation be for their repentive (new word) hearts. Amen.

Christopher A. Wray, America is watching you. Mr. Wray, what would JESUS do? Your treasure is where the heart is. JESUS explained why one should store one's treasure in Heaven rather than on earth. In your case, rather than with the corrupted top-level government official like yourself.

Do the will of GOD the Father. [128]"And this is the will of Him who sent Me, that everyone who sees the Son and believes in Him may have everlasting life; and I will raise him up at the last day." Do not miss your opportunity to make JESUS your Lord.

I saw JESUS, He appeared to me, therefore; I give testimony as a witness that GODISJESUSLIVES. Amen. GODISJESUSLIVES. Amen.

The devil wants you to focus on yourself, or as I say y'allselves (new word), wanting you to focus on your obedience and not what matters, JESUS' obedience on the cross blessing all of us. All thoughts and actions go towards the obedience of CHRIST JESUS. Praise GOD for loving us. And all glory goes to GOD in and through CHRIST JESUS.

I try to give thanks to GOD every morning by saying, "I thank you GOD in and through JESUS CHRIST for giving me another day to worship You, to glorify You, to praise You, To serve You and Love You. Amen." I do speak to JESUS daily. We have rights through the obedience of JESUS.

Humble yourself and have faith in the gospel, the good news of GOD. Boast in JESUS CHRIST and in Him alone. Become a Christian, a follower of CHRIST JESUS. Is GOD your GOD?

---

[128] John 6:39

GOD is just. JESUS is our Savior and willing that any one of us should parish, but that all of us come to repentance. The Lord isn't really being slow about his promise, as some people think. No, He is being patient for your sake. He does not want anyone to be destroyed, but wants everyone to repent. JESUS wants everyone to be saved and to understand the truth.

Soon GOD is sending His Son, Lord JESUS, for us believers. JESUS second coming is as King to judge this fallen world. King JESUS will rule this earth, purge and clean this earth. There will be a new Heaven and a new earth. "Then I saw a new heaven and a new earth, for the old heaven and the old earth had disappeared. And the sea was also gone." JESUS tells us this, entire. Do not be alarmed, if you are saved, born again, a believer. JESUS is coming to save us believers

As I write this, my love for JESUS grows and grows. My faith in JESUS strengthens. My desire to leave this world surpasses all things. I see Him. I dance with Him after fellowship to a wonderful spiritual song of Joseph Prince. I see the holes in JESUS hands. My love for JESUS is first. Fellow Christians at my level y'all know what I speak of. I desire salvation for all, even the most wrenched of GODS children. I hate lucifer, evil angels and demons, all darkness.

JESUS is brilliant. He always tells me what to answer my husband with. My husband always angers me with his own interpretation of law and lack of Grace as he did again last night. I told him there is no judgment for JESUS boys and girls, believers in JESUS.

Steve replied, "oh I guess you can do whatever you want to then Yvonne." He wouldn't even aloe me to explain to him that when you are born again in CHRIST JESUS you want to please GOD. You don't want to hurt JESUS. You don't want to steal, kill, commit sexual immorality and other sins, which hurt our LORD GOD.

If you marry your partner of the same sex, then you are seeking attention in this fading world. JESUS dislikes the sin, sexual immorality. A person is not born that way. They choose that life style for attention.

Learn to say no to the demons whispering in your ear to give into your evil flesh. I love watching "Peter and Paul" starring Robert Foxworth (Peter) and Anthony Hopkins (Paul of Tarsas). It is Hopkins best acting, directed well, and a movie JESUS led me to. It is too bad he will forever be remembered as a cannibal, but that is not as damning as Jodie Foster's eternal abode if she does not repent. She may believe in JESUS, I don't know, but she is wise enough to know she will not enter the

Kingdom of GOD unless she repents, which means quit your sexual immorality by choosing the same sex. Ellen DeGeneres, you too will have eternity to think about your ill choice while torment is your abode unless you choose JESUS and repentance. All sexual immoral people will have eternity to regret.[129]"Neither was man created for woman, but woman for man."

Don't you know,[130]"that the unrighteous will not inherit the Kingdom of GOD? Do not be deceived: neither the sexually immoral, nor idolaters, nor adulters, nor men who practice homosexuality, nor thieves, nor the greedy, nor drunkards, nor revilers, nor swindlers will inherit the Kingdom of GOD."

---

[129] 1Corinthians 11:9

[130] 1Corinthians 6:9-10

[131]"For this reason GOD gave them up to dishonorable passions. For their women exchanged natural relations for those that are contrary to nature; and the men likewise gave up natural relations with women and were consumed with passion for one another, men committing shameless acts with men and receiving in themselves the due penalty for their error. And since they did not see fit to acknowledge GOD, GOD gave them up to a debased mind to do what ought not to be done." Its all fun and games right now Anderson Cooper. Repent you so Damned and Gaymoras. Repent! Do you want to burn for eternity after death on earth? Think about truth.

This morning, JESUS said to tell Steve that when one of the thief next to Him on the cross, said to the other thief, to quit complaining and quite down that, they deserved the punishment for what they had done…JESUS said, the thief was repenting at that very moment.

Further, the saved thief said to JESUS to remember him when JESUS "came into His Kingdom…" that was belief in JESUS as the Son of GOD, the Savior, the Messiah. Repentance and belief was the action by the thief on the cross, which led to salvation and told to me first by JESUS this morning (May 11, 2018). JESUS didn't say ok but first let me judge you now that you are born again. Lol. That is not Grace. My dear husband understood, again. Amazing is our LORD GOD. That is my JESUS. Wow again that JESUS said the thief on the cross next to Him repented and believed that very moment.[132]"JESUS remember me when You come into Your Kingdom."

---

[131] Romans 1:26-28

[132] Luke 23:42

Father, in Your name JESUS I pray all hate aimed towards Your son Donald, his family and those he loves and prays for bounces off him and lands on those haters. Continue to shower the entire Trump family with Grace upon Grace and unmerited favor upon favor and a sphere of protection. Amen.

I understand what Joyce Myers means when she says JESUS gave her, her childhood back her, her 50's and 60's...the LORD GOD taught me how to be child like all over again from reminding me to brush my teeth, wash my face, shower every night, wipe, wash correctly, even wanting to have more 5's than Joseph Prince.

Finding the number of Grace in my life is a serious happening between JESUS and me. 604 Power Street, 78377, childhood address; June 20, 1964, birthday; 512-526-2606 family phone number; 45012 2709 social security; 406 249 0046 cell phone; 406 309 0855 (hotspot phone number I got yesterday, June 13, 2018); I graduated from Refugio High School in 1982; I cried to GOD, but my drivers license does not equal a sum of 5, JESUS said, "divide it by 5" MT driver's license number ?601?1964?120 divided by 5 = 0120243928824, I said that's nice but it still did not sum 5, 5, etc., JESUS said, "add it now" well it is now the sum of 45. in addition to the many times Grace is upon me. Lol. I Love You JESUS! My social security number is the sum of 30. My cell number = the sum of 20. 5 goes on and on in my life. Just noting the number of Grace upon me! JESUS anoints me everyday and I am doing what He has called me to do.

Joseph Prince knows...I learned 5 number of Grace watching one of his sermons. JESUS tickles me a lot. JESUS dances with me. Puts a smile on my face. I could go on and on.

On a more serious note: My husband smokes pot, smoked it, hate it. I am clean as a whistle so to speak. His excuse to me is that it is legal and he has a legal card. JESUS immediately told me to tell him prostitution is legal in Brussels Belgium but it is a sinful act. Wow! JESUS is a Man of few words and quick to answer.

It was my gateway to meth, the drug of choice. Hate it all, including alcohol. Costing me relationships. I love my family. I love my brother, my two sisters and all my aunts and uncles, nieces and nephews, cousin and in-laws, from the beginning of time throughout eternity.

I want to apologize to the best husband a women can ask for. Sorry Greg for being a terrible wife, you were the best thing ever happened to me before I was saved and born again. Having you Greg led to our daughter, the love of my life in the flesh. I did ask him to forgive me over a decade ago. Breaking our family apart was the worst mistake of my life; however that mistake has led me to a path into the Kingdom of GOD. I willfully chose repentance and JESUS.

The most sorry I am is for the way I have hurt "Cookie" Ina Jean Metty, a true daughter of GOD in all aspects spiritually and in the flesh. Never have I met and never will I meet again, a person who is true to JESUS. I cannot put into words how true blue she is as a Christian and sister in CHRIST. She forgave me before I ever asked. I have hurt my dear friend in more ways than any one else on earth and for that I am truly sorry. I did not have the honors of meeting "Jan" Janice Wendell Crouch (JESUS told me), but Cookie is of the same mold, rare. I love you Cookie. Credit is given to the best photographer I know, Cookie took the picture used by JESUS for the cover of this book. JESUS who told me to use this picture for the cover. Father, in Your name JESUS I pray Grace beyond all given ever before to any Child of Yours for Cookie, my family and all those I and we love and pray for. Amen.

My name is written in the "Lambs Book of Life." I do want to say that his feathered bed I slept in while visiting our daughter in Scottsdale while he was away flying commercial airplane (his occupation) was the best bed I ever slept on. Feathered pillows are what I use and are the best pillows ever. Another serious note: Sorry Chad for the horrible person I was under the influence of meth. You're the best son in law a mother could ever ask GOD for. I have paid an irreversible price for my mistakes in life. Forgive me.

Find a church that preachers and teaches the Gospel of Grace. You do not want to associate yourself with a religion that is founded on the Old Covenant Ten Commandment. Are you a Christian or are you a Jehovah Witness? One unforgiving sin is denying the Holy Spirit. If you blaspheme the Holy Spirit you Jehovah Witnesses and luciferian company you have already been judged, [133]it is an unforgivable sin. The church is the bride if JESUS. We are what comprise His bride. Get in a good Gospel of Grace bible teaching church. Don't choose non-denominational church (even non-denominational is a denomination) unless they profess they are and do teach from the Holy Bible, the Gospel of Grace.

---

[133] Mark 3:28-30

I know what it is like to be loved by JESUS. I know what it is like to have the spirit of fear leave your body forever. I know what it is like to feel glorious divineness presence in the same room with you. I know what it feels like to have JESUS' holy angels take charge of me. I know what it feels like to have the Almighty GOD call you daughter. I know what it feels like to have GOD tell you that you shall be a "judge." I know what it feels like to have JESUS tell you don't worry you shall be delivered "swiftly." I know what it feels like to have JESUS tell you, "compassion." I know what it feels like to have GOD'S angels surround you and not allow you to leave the premise while evil lurked through flesh and blood to hurt you. I know what it feels like to have JESUS appear. I know what it feels like to see JESUS carry the cross in His real time during Pontius Pilate crucifixion. I know what it feels like to see the angels celebrate JESUS defeat of death on the Cross. I know what it feels like to have your name written in the "Lamb's Book of Life." I know what it feels like to know I will attend at the LORD'S Wedding Supper to come. I know what it feels like to speak to JESUS who is GOD. I know what it feels like to have GOD'S Glory surround you at all times and seal you with His name. I know what it feels like to be born again, to have salvation. I know what it is like to be in this world. I know what it is like to no longer fear man. I know what it is like to be humbled. I know what it is like to love all without thought or effort. I know what it is like to hate evil only. I know what it feels like to have your military daughter return from an Iraqi tour. I know what it feels like to be the righteousness of GOD in CHRIST. I know what it feels like to be sanctified by JESUS. I know what it feels like to be anointed by JESUS.

I know what it feels like to speak to the devil. I know what it feels like to be tormented by hundreds of demons at once. I know what it feels like to be tricked by them. I know what it feels like to be evil. I know what it feels like to believe and know there is a JESUS, but not repent, not change my ways, continue down my way of being evil. I know what it is like to be of this world. I know what it is like to idolize money. I know what it is like to be scared of flesh and blood. I know what it feels like to be unwhite (new word). I know what it feels like to be bullied. I know what it feels like to be made fun of until you cry. I know pain. I know what it feels like to be left out. I know what it feels like to be laughed at by your classmates. I know what it feels like to be brown skin. I know what it feels like to be exiled. I know what it feels like to be forced something your not. I know what it feels like to be called a marrano, a pig. I know what it feels like to be labeled. I know what it feels like to be a minority. I know what it feels like to grow up in a n all white community. I know what it feels like to be discriminated against. I know hat it feels like to be near death at the hands of another. I know what it feels like to be surrounded by drug dealers who were sent there to kill you. I know what it feels like to sleep with the enemy. I know what it feels like to steal, cheat, kill (abortions) and a liar. I know what it feels like to starve. I know what it feels like to have a person in your house lay his 45 handgun on your desk out of respect, then go on a cop run, shot and killed on TV live. I know what it feels like to hate. I know what it feels like to live with hundreds of mice and no windows or electricity. I know. I know what it feels like to be blind. I know what it feels like to be seconds from death and gasping for life. I know what it feels like to have your military daughter leave for an Iraqi tour.

The rapture is going to happen within 14 years from now and I was told this directly from JESUS. I was told May of 2032 is significant, but believers will already be caught up in the clouds with JESUS and before Armageddon. I relay this information to you from Our LORD GOD JESUS. JESUS said no one knows the day or hour but He did not say the month or year. That was the first thing I said to JESUS and He corrected me with scripture,[134] "But about that day or hour no one knows, not even the angels in heaven, nor the Son, but only the Father...Therefore you also must be ready, for the Son of Man is coming at an hour you do not expect."

GOD the Father did tell Peter JESUS was the CHRIST.[135]" JESUS replied, blessed are you, Simon son of Jonah, for this was not revealed to you by flesh and blood, but my Father in Heaven." Don't wait give yourself to JESUS now!!! Now! This book is about JESUS and not about me. It's all about JESUS. Amen.

JESUS revealed to me, May 2032 is 14 years from now. President Trump 2018- 2020 is 2 years, 2020-2024 is another 4 years, then President Trump's predecessor 2024-2032 is 8 years, totaling 14 years. Five is the number of GOD'S Grace; Multiplied by itself is Grace upon Grace. Five, GOD' S Grace is a symbol of GODS goodness and favor toward flesh and blood and mentioned 318 times in the Holy Bible. 2032 divided by 5 = 4064...4+6+4 is 14 years from now. 2032 = 7 the number of GOD perfection. 2032 divided by five 0032 = 5 number of Grace. Only GOD knows the "day or hour." Mark 13:32 and Matthew 24:36 in the Gospel of Grace.

If you are not with us JESUS boys and girls then you are against us and you are children of the devil. luciferians are you all. All areas of this world is fallen to lucifer, the created fallen angel satan, the deceiver.

---

[134] Matthew 24:36-44; 1Thessalonians 5:1-3; Peter 3:10; Revelation

[135] Matthew 16:17

The wrath of GOD is going to be poured out on those that chose evil satan. In all of GOD dealing with the human race, the nation of Israel is at the center of it all. The deceiver, satan hates what GOD loves.

Bottom line, repent, believe and call His name for help. Call on JESUS. Call JESUS. GODISJESUSLIVES. Amen.

NOTES FROM VISIONS

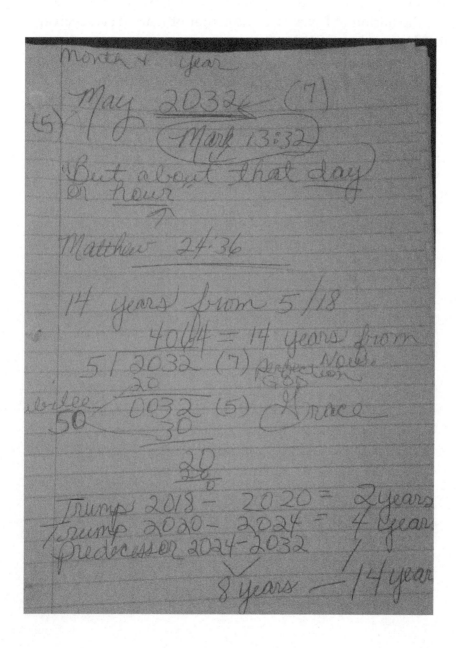

> Cactus Buckley
>
> my Toothbrush container
> 1st Vision
>
> 3/18 Vision march 18 19
>
> 2 hours — antichrist
>
> fall off edge of bed. i got light and late fever edge gone completely gone — nowhere to be found. Revelation 13:1
>
> Vision 3/18/18
>
> Trump & Roger De Coster from Belgium
> USA — Crowned as king made a Knight
> 2nd Vision — United Nations
>
> Vision 03/18/2018
>
> first rock — unable to crack
> second rock — unable to crack
> 3rd rock in my hand peels/crumbles off
> "Brilliant" "Lazul"
> "Victorious" Sapphire
> Kingdom is GOD's Throne

JESUS said,

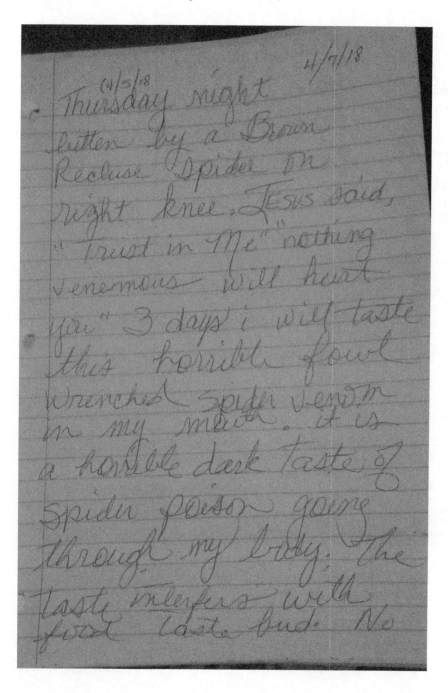

(4/5/18) 4/7/18

Thursday night bitten by a Brown Recluse Spider on right knee. Jesus said, "Trust in Me" "nothing venemous will hurt you" 3 days i will taste this horrible foul wrenched spider venom in my mouth. it is a horrible dark taste of spider poison going through my body. The taste interferes with food taste bud. No

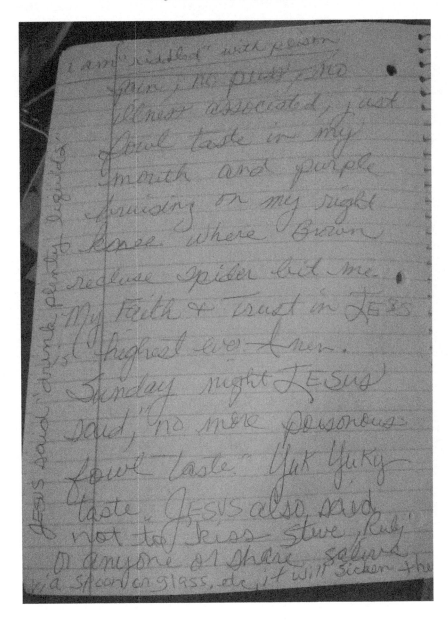

i am "riddled" with poison pain, no pus, no illness associated, just foul taste in my mouth and purple bruising on my right knee where Brown recluse spider bit me. My Faith & Trust in JESUS is highest ever Amen. Sunday night JESUS said, "no more poisonous foul taste." Yuk Yuky taste. JESUS also said, not to kiss Steve, Ruby or anyone or share saliva via spoon or glass, etc, it will sicken th—

Jesus said "drunk plenty liquids"

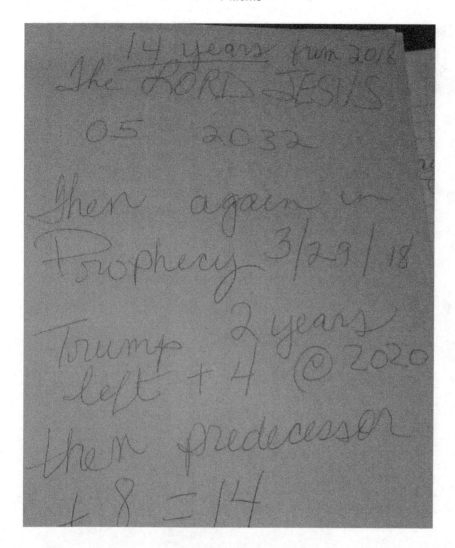

"Daughter, No One Called My Name"

PICTURES OF AN UNSAVED GIRL.

Our Lady of Refuge school picture, I'm the dark girl, second row, and right corner side bottom next to Mrs. Bauer (awesome lady and family-Hi Kurt!) sitting in chair.

Our Lady of Refuge Catholic School, I am the very dark little girl;
Me and Mom;
Blackie, my first dog and Me.

Muhammad Ali

Black Beach on Maui

"Daughter, No One Called My Name"

Mom and Me;
Daughter and Me;

Clint Eastwood

"Daughter, No One Called My Name"

Paco and Me

"Daughter, No One Called My Name"

My Mom and Dad;
My "Jitterbug" Niece and Me;
My Fe' Fe' daughter and Me.

Made in the USA
Middletown, DE
14 April 2024

52943631R00096